From the Ground Up

FROM THE GROUND UP

OVERCOME THE PAST AND REBUILD YOUR CONFIDENCE

TAMMY JO
FOUNDER OF BREAKING GROUND LEARNING SYSTEMS & CHANGING FUTURE OUTCOMES EXPERT

SELF PUBLISHED THROUGH CREATE SPACE

Copyright © [2014] - [Tammy Jo]

[Breaking Ground Learning Systems and Tammy Jo]
The moral right of the author has been asserted.

All rights reserved.

Unless otherwise indicated, all scripture quotations are from The Holy Bible, New International Version at
http://www.biblegateway.com/versions/New-International-Version-NIV-Bible/

No part of this publication may be reproduced, stored in a retrieval system, or transmitted, in any form or by any means, without the prior permission in writing of the publisher, nor be otherwise circulated in any form of binding or cover other than that in which it is published and without a similar condition including this condition being imposed on the subsequent purchaser.

Every effort has been made to ensure that the information contained in this book is complete and accurate. However the author is not engaged in rendering professional advice or services to the individual reader. The ideas, assignments and suggestions contained in this book are not intended as a substitute for consulting with your physician or therapist. All matters regarding your physical or mental health require proper medical supervision. Neither the author nor the publisher shall be liable or responsible for any loss, injury, or damage allegedly arising from any information or suggestion in this book. The opinions expressed in this book represent the personal views of the author.

Due to the nature of this book, names and situations have been slightly modified to protect the identity of other individuals.

Self Published by [Breaking Ground Learning Systems c/o Tammy Jo]
For permission requests, write to the publisher at the address below:

P.O. BOX 583 Westerville, Ohio 43086

Ordering Information:

For details, contact the publisher at the address above.
Orders by U.S. trade bookstores and wholesalers. Please contact: Tel: 1-(855)275-1187; or email tammyjo@tammyjojohnson.com

The author is not responsible for websites (or their content) that are not owned by the publisher

Manufactured in the United States of America

Cover artwork designed by
e-sourcemedia.com
ISBN-13: 978-0615976402

Typesetting services by BOOKOW.COM

To My Mom:

There was a time that every thought of you made me cry. There was a time that life had no meaning for me and I just didn't want to live it without you.

I was so scared that I would never find reason enough to go on and live my life because you were not here.

If you were here, I would tell you thank you for being the best mom in the whole world.

Thank you for your love, care and discipline.

It's because of you that I love my daughter so much that I sometimes smother her. Thank you for teaching me how to protect.

It's because of you that it's not a big deal when my son brings home an average grade in English but an A in math. Thank you for teaching me balance.

It's because of you that I gave birth to my youngest son and decided that starting over would be way more fun than the guilt of "wondering". Thank you for teaching me patience.

It's because of you that I have three beautiful children

who love me so much that leaving this world without seeing them through theirs would tear them apart. I see so much of you in me that I understand now, some of the feelings you went through and the reasons why you did the things you did.

But it's your love I feel the most because that love is so strong that I feel your forgiveness and not only does it ground me, gives me confidence and foundation—it grows me.

Thank you for giving me the truth, that I will see you again someday but knowing for now...

I have work to do.

Thank you for being my reason to live.

"For I know the plans I have for you," declares the Lord, "plans to prosper you and not to harm you, plans to give you hope and a future.

–Jeremiah 29:11

Holy Bible -NIV

Contents

Acknowledgements	1
Introduction	7
How to Read This Book	15
Part One – The Story	23
Chapter One – The Nightmare on My Street	25
Chapter Two – Handle the Truth with Care	41
Chapter Three – My Life. My View.	49
Chapter Four – Bullied and Taunted	53
Chapter Five – Dream Anxiety Disorder	59
Conclusion of Part One	67
Part Two – The Transition	69
Chapter Six – Wait. She Did What?	71
Chapter Seven – YOU. Under Construction	77
Chapter Eight – Confidence is for Parenting	79
Chapter Nine – The Silent War Against Parents	91
Chapter Ten – Taking Back Our Parental Authority	97
Chapter Eleven – Why Parents Need Trained in Confidence	101
Chapter Twelve – Confidence is for Individuality	119
Chapter Thirteen – Confidence is for Relationships	147
Chapter Fourteen – Confidence Eliminates Bullying	163
Chapter Fifteen – Confidence in Fear	175
Conclusion of Part Two	179

Part Three – The "Grounded in Confidence" Platform	181
Chapter Sixteen – Tools for Rebuilding Confidence	183
Chapter Seventeen – Roadblocks Ahead	191
Epilogue	201

Acknowledgements

God gets all firsts.

I acknowledge Him in all my personal and business endeavours because He is Lord of my life. Duh. Right? If not for His love, grace and son Jesus Christ, I would have no real explanation for why I came through hell unburned and fumeless.

I HATE religion. It serves no real purpose.

This is why I kept this book out of *that* section. Not because I don't want people to label me as Christian, but because a lot of us have gone completely crazy religious. The last thing I want is to be boxed or labelled.

If God doesn't "box" me, no one else can.

I'm very clear on who I am. This is a blessing and sometimes feels like a curse.

I am a Spirit that lives in a body. I have a soul. Spirits don't do boxes. That being said, I AM a Christian. My faith and a few examples in this book are based off of biblical principles and ideas. My forgiveness, peace, and limitless love towards others are encased within my "relationship" with Jesus Christ. If you don't believe in

God right now or you are straddling the fence, hopefully you have an idea of how He works before you're done reading this book. I always tell people:

"I'd rather trust in my innate wisdom and live this life accountably, with a God-driven platform, embraced in love and relationship rather than living unaccountably, vicariously in a realm with half-baked ideas about evolution only to die, learn that I was wrong, and be too late to choose. It's a win win."

To try and acknowledge every person who shined light into my darkness or spoke life into the death that devoured my soul would be a book in and of itself. Those people know who they are.

Then there are those who have had a profound impact and influence on my life and I get to thank them here. That's one of the cool perks of writing a book.

Therefore,

Dr. David C. Forbes Jr: As a teenager, you embraced and invited me into your church, home and heart. You led and trained me properly in the things of God and made the journey seamless. You did not judge me based on a file, idea, or crime. Your love and dedication to my God-purpose melted the hardness off my heart. From chasing away boys, to shooting hoops, you are the dad that I never had. If it were not for your spiritual guidance and availability, I would not know what a father or husband is supposed to look like. I thank God for you every time I overcome an obstacle, reach a goal …or date a guy. I always hear you say "I'm already proud of you". I will always love, honor, and appreciate you. **Thank you for my "new foundation".**

Acknowledgements

Dr. Tracy Forbes: From the time I met you, I watched you. I may not have said much verbally (unless I was in distress), but you were my moral paradigm. I studied you as a woman, a mom, and a wife because of your beauty and God-like character. I then practiced those behaviors and characteristics until they became mine. Every time you offered wisdom and direction, my teenage actions may have portrayed one thing, but your words were received and engraved in my spirit. I will always love, honor, and appreciate you. **Thank you for being my illustration of a "captivating woman".**

Lavonne Bailey & Ronda Hughes & Family: I know that holiday gatherings are taken for granted by most, but for me, every Christmas and Thanksgiving in your home became my "family" prototype. For my existent behaviour and the way I handle myself a woman with kids, thank you for your discipline and direction. For my mature (and often complimented by others) character, thank you for your influence and wisdom. For the authenticity of my heart, thank you for your consistent and anchored love. Our God-ordained alliance could not have been more custom-made for me. I will always love, honor, and appreciate you. **Thank you for teaching me family and for being mine.**

Pastors Keith & Melanie Bradley: You have walked alongside and loved me through the toughest and darkest phases of my life. You've seen my tears, listened to my dreams and ideas, and prayed with me the most. I have always admired and drew wisdom from your effortless availability and "tell-it-like-it-is" counsel in a crazy-busy ministry. You patiently taught and influenced my parenting, creativity, and tolerance. You encouraged the freedom of my "me-ness", while consistently reaffirming my Godly purpose. Because of you, my transition from adolescence into womanhood was strong and humble. I will always love, honor, and appreciate you (while packing and booking my flight). **Thank you for coaching my religion into relationship.** My bold and transparent authenticity was bred by you.

Chelsea Azille: Surrounded by sound discipline and accountability made me appreciate our rebellion. I thank God for 'restoring back my youth' through our adventurous friendship. The uninhibited career that involved flying around the country, the ridiculousness of living homeless on the streets of Los Angeles, and the irresponsibility of getting stranded in New Mexico were the best highlights of my life. You have seen me through heartbreak and divorce, multiple day road trips, and graduated broadcasting school alongside of me. You "became" my best friend later in life, but you and I will always have the tangled soul of a childhood friendship. You are loyal, consistent, and irreplaceable. I will always love, honor, and appreciate you. **No matter what this life has for our individual destinations, I will always love and accept you. You will always be my "lifetime best friend".**

Marci Sutherland & Gwendolyn Shealey: As a child, being thrown into an already dangerous system, there could have easily been room for foul play. There were at least four attempts you deliberately hijacked: Hypnosis experiments, psychological diagnosis, sexual misconduct, and media abuse. It takes a very special person to really care about the (delayed or invisible) difference that you make through dedication and commitment. As I got older, I took on character traits, professionalism and "best practices" that you demonstrated by example. You taught me independence and inner structure while building and exchanging trust with me. When it was time to begin the process of healing, you were my padded walls. I will always love, honor, and appreciate you. Thank you for "protecting" and "cultivating" my adolescence.

Jamaul Smith: Your friendship couldn't have come at a better time. You liberated me from my own fear. A simple laugh, long, late conversation and the pure simplicity of friendship is rare. Having someone around to agree with, understand, brainstorm and relate with authentically is priceless. I don't know what life ahead looks like for us, but I am pretty convinced it will be special. You are the very reason why I now understand the clarity between standard definition (SD) and high definition (HD) television. Even humble beginnings can cause major impact. **I will always appreciate you and be there.** I honor you for being the man you are. Thank you for being "clear" during my cloudy time. –Lois.

Introduction

I shot my mom when I was twelve-years-old during a premeditated attempt to commit suicide. The darkness of the living room, my lack of experience with the firearm, along with the poisonous family secrets that penetrated my soul caused my inability to tell the difference between nightmares and reality. That confusion created massive destruction that altered the rest of my life.

I wish this second paragraph was all about my mom's forgiveness and my new understanding of unhealthy secrets. I would take everything I felt emotionally and lay it all out on the table for somebody—anybody—to help me sort through it.

You see, I was her only little girl.

Yet I'm also responsible for her death.

When I would think back to that horrible night, I'd be so overwhelmed with remorse that it drowned me into depression. Trying to wrap my mind around the intervention of the empty safety chamber of the gun that was supposed to end something—yet changed everything—was useless and disheartening. For years I felt guilty and misplaced in my own life. She wasn't supposed to die, I was.

As I got older, I negotiated if settling the score would complete the mission. I felt like I didn't deserve to live after that, no matter how much I healed or had forgiven myself. I felt like I'd lost that right.

I've attempted to write this book for the past six years, wanting to help others without revealing anything about my past in fear that my future would be tampered with. I wanted an effective way to help other people overcome their past without revealing too much of mine. I wanted to inspire and reassure that joy can dominate defeat. When I realized that leaving out my story defeated the point, I laid to rest the vision of omittance. That concept or behavior didn't last long. Nothing I did ever satisfied my zeal and appreciation for life. Until now.

Talking about it was even harder when I first started to coach others. I learned quickly that voluntarily exposing the skeletons in my room (yeah, the closets were too small) – caused all skeletons alike to be exposed. Those people were empowered because I exemplified hope.

This catastrophe, along with other harrowing life events, ratified the amount of freedom that is given with releasing secrets. Speaking out about being sexually molested and how I really felt about being bullied, released extreme relief. The freedom of bondage was exhilarating because the secrets no longer held power once they were revealed. Once I began shedding light on them, they became subject to a community of other like-secrets where healing and overcoming took place.

I realized that I wasn't alone.

I had to make a decision to create my own philosophy about my life. Then, hold myself accountable for the steps it would take to

Introduction

put that philosophy into practice. For as long as I could remember no one else cared about how my life would turn out. No one was truly invested in my future except my mom. When I realized that I was the only one left out of the two of us who would care, it became my responsibility, so I took action.

In my first plan of action, I thought about, evaluated, and controlled what I was saying about myself. I got rid of phrases like, "I will never be able to", "If that would have never happened " and "It's too late for me". In other words, my words profoundly impacted my capabilities.

Here is one of those "I-never-thought-about-it-like-that" conclusions:

Your mouth is closest to your ears. When words verbally travel in that short of a distance they are more potent as opposed to the distance of hearing them from someone else.

In other words, my verbalization about *me* had a stronger impact on *my life's* results. I chose to move forward in confidence. My self-worth as a leader, parent, and individual and was measured against that determination. Don't get me wrong, "affirmations" are only the beginning of overcoming. Affirmations are the easiest thing to do, but they are the hardest habit to create. One of my favorite speakers, Eric Thomas, said this:

"You cannot talk yourself out of something you behaved yourself into".

This is both uncomfortable and true. My results did not appear from positive speaking alone. I had to eventually take action...a lot of action. Next, I listened. I was fortunate to have verbal influences in my life that told me I mattered. I had people in my adult life that loved me regardless of my performance, behavior, understanding, or distance. It was those people who knew what I had been through, but got to know me as an individual. I chose to believe in what they saw *in* me, until the smoke cleared from my own vision. Most would call this "intervention".

Reading a story like this and watching my life unfold with the knowledge of all the obstacles I have overcome will have a powerful impact on your life. Knowing that my mess didn't destroy me, might be the only message you need to believe that the mess in your life doesn't have to destroy you either.

Most would call this "inspiration".

From the Ground Up, and the design of it, was created with you (my reader) in mind. It's not about *me* per se. I am the result. I have high self- confidence and establish new levels of confidence all the time as a result of the practices and habits I introduce to you. Because of this learned confidence, you don't have to struggle your way through what I have already overcome. I offer you the shortcuts and the results. I'm offering you the blueprint of how I rebuilt my life and changed my expected outcome so that you have instruction for yourself and can then equip others. This domino effect can transform future generations. However, we need to start some place—together.

Most would call this building a "community".

I'm not twelve-years-old anymore. I can move forward without the guilt and shame of what I cannot change.

I honor and appreciate God so much for the way He strategically and purposefully coated me in forgiveness and love. I continue to

Introduction

be in awe of the healing that transforms my life every day. It's like; He detached my wounded heart from its chambers and re-attached His. I'd be satisfied to live the rest of my life wrapped in His grace and the freedom of His peace.

But I can't.

That's not why I'm here. I did not come through darkness and defeat for my own purpose. I'm here because you need to know that you are not alone. I want to extend to you my rare, exclusive authority and permission to step out in your "YOU-ness" regardless of what has been done to you that may have affected your life negatively. I like to think of myself as an example of a modern day David or Peter. It keeps my confidence in check when I want to ask for forgiveness for the same thing over and over. I also want you, my reader, to be able to say,

"Wow, if she could make it through THAT, I can most certainly make it through this."

I don't promise you an error free, super polished, best-selling book of seven habits. What I promise you is my voice. I was bullied, so I will EXPOSE what it really feels like when you are hereditarily different and can't walk the halls of middle school without harassment. I will also verbalize how corporate America is a lot like middle school.

I was repeatedly molested; therefore, I will EXPOSE the elephant in the room so that you know that you're not the only one who sees it. I will verbalize the discomfort of family secrets that destroys lives so that maybe you can make sure your family is free of those.

I was very depressed as a child, that I destructively held myself hostage. Therefore, I will be the VOICE of reason for your negotiation in depression and help you to dis-wire very carefully. I will help you see the perspectives that you have been blinded to.

My overcomers' blueprint is based on raw, uncut, and transparent experiences. I am a results expert. Everything that is mastery for me, I will certify and see you through. I am also a life learner. I will introduce you to alternatives and updates.

Connecting the dots of my life in reverse, every hardship, every lesson and every test (passed or failed) has led me *here*. I am sealed, stamped, and certified to lead you on this self-reflective journey. You will conquer the victim mentality that has kept you from being who you are truly meant to be and begin the life you deserve. I have the gathered the tools that you need to overcome the past and rebuild your confidence and self-worth. The same tools that rebuilt me.

This journey is unbiased and voluntary. It is also foundational. I won't leave out important pieces of the foundation to satisfy everyone's desire, nor will I edit truth to fit a genre. I will however support and you can customize.

That being said;

Yes, I am a Christian and I finally get what the difference is between having a relationship with Jesus and performing in religion for the world. My life wouldn't make any real sense without my faith so I will never omit that or water it down.

But this is not that book.

Introduction

I love fictional humor and lighthearted stories surrounding life, lemons, and lemonade. I've made tons of jars –probably to the point of wholesale and distribution.

But this... is not that book.

It is awesome-cool the way agents and major publishers take a story and make it marketable to its target audience, free of grammar errors and word misplacement, making it flawless and perfect. As a creative writer, I would love to experience that one day, but unfortunately,

This is not that book either.

I am a thirty-six-year-old "momtrepenuer". (My version of the word)

I am an imperfect-perfect-version-in-this-season-of-my-life-me.

I can navigate through all the chaos in this world without losing my "ME-ness". That fearlessness used to be reckless and out-of-control. It is now balanced.

I am one of the best, loving parents on the planet, but I still yell at my kids and secretly disappear to the basement or lock myself in the bathroom when I want some alone time (Yes, one is a teenager).

The dishwasher distracts me from completing the laundry, so most of the time neither gets done. I refuse to potty train with pull-ups, I'd rather text than talk, I tried to take on the career of a stripper (not realizing that knowing how to dance was a requirement) and more often than I'd like to admit, I've searched frantically for my cell phone, while on it. I have been diagnosed with adult ADHD (Go figure).

I am real.

However, I have overcome some of life's hell hot obstacles without blistering burns or smelly smoke, I am irritatingly happy all the time, I am divorced and not bitter, I can make a positive spin on anything, I used to be considered "ugly" by others' standards, but have been a spokes model for some of the top commercial brands, I consistently redefine "rare-beauty" and most importantly, I've been there, done that and still have the permit.

I am an official, never-before-seen results driven guru that will help you get off your butt, discover your gifts and talents, re-establish your foundational confidence and get you about the business of your real life's purpose–like I did mine.

So, if you dare to begin this journey while reading a series of disturbing-yet-true, sarcastically humorous yet-effective stories about how I rebuilt my confidence with overcoming and winning as the end result—from the ground up,

Then–

This is that book.

How to Read This Book

Around publishing time, after the manuscript was complete, I wanted to place a large disclosure stamp on the cover that says:

WARNING: THIS IS NOT A MEMOIR

But instead, I decided to include directions on how to read this book (you will understand why after the first few chapters).

From the Ground Up has a self-help exhortation and a personal development principle in a memoir environment. The intent is to start you from the beginning and walk along side of you through the dysfunction of my life explaining key issues and pointing out relevant dialog. I tried, for a long time, to write a book on establishing this confidence without the story of how mine came into existence.

That never worked.

The structure of *From the Ground Up* is unique within heart of the pages because I get the opportunity to tell you my story as the woman I am today. I get to utilize my creative communication to speak out against the situations that were supposed to destroy me so that you will recognize the destruction of some of your situations, and have a heads up. You get to see firsthand that my personality, character and heart don't fit the brokenness of my past experiences.

Which is what makes it compelling.

Perhaps a large publishing firm would've given better direction in the areas of grammar and organization making this a truly remarkable manuscript. I even hope to offer some direction to you when you're ready to write your story. Thing is, you don't need another standard to try and live up to. Besides, our children, leaders, and communities needed this information yesterday.

I'm already late.

While professionalism was ideal, it's also subjective. It's more important to offer you a not-so-perfectly-written, but authentically understood book that makes you laugh, relates to your life, and has the ability to save your marriage, job or children. It's more important to set the example of what I am encouraging you to do. Self-publish away I say!

The structural development of this book consists of three main sections; *The Story*, *The Transition*, and the introduction to the first of five series titled, *Grounded in Confidence*, which is the *From the Ground Up* training platform.

The Story- Is just that. I began with the night that changed my life forever. I work my way forward from there. I bring you into my childhood through my eyes *now* with feelings of *then*. I then share my way of thinking along with some snarky-ness for enlightenment and humor. I was so torn and trapped by life. I knew then that something was wrong, I just didn't know *what*. Utilizing humor helps to break away from the heaviness of the subject.

Although not in chronological order, I remember a lot of details about my life surrounding different times when I was being abused, bullied or molested. I also remember how I felt during most of those horrid experiences and believe that you will be able to relate. Now that I am able to adequately express those feelings, I can teach you how to do the same. Nothing allows for faster healing like being able to give expression to feelings about the abuse that we encountered in the past–unapologetically. I had to pull out a few old journals, letters and reports and conduct some interviews to tie things together, but the point is to offer transparency.

This is also where I give a little insight on what my life inside of the institution was like. I share a few stories and teach you what my "uninterrupted" learning environment looked like as I *grew up on the inside*.

The Transition is a shift to take you from the institutional mentality that I was told I would never shake, to my real life experience once I was released. I talk about some of the issues I faced as a result of being away from a normal environment for so long and how I adapted. I explain the mentality that came along with leaving one system trained to step into another one and how I figured out how to break the cycle. I give you the philosophy and psychology around healthy self-esteem and confidence and why it's foundation to all other areas of life. In this part of *From the Ground Up*, I also give you my *reason* why I want to help others and a little overview of how I plan to with the series of books and eBook's that will follow.

My hope is that everything zooms into focus for you. Telling my story in this format makes me more of a real person you can relate with. I am a woman, parent and leader with similar issues as other women, parents and leaders. When I understood my role in this expert space, I knew that getting to know me as a person then author would be better received. I am a servant at heart. I may not have superpowers and be able to change everyone's life—but I do have a plan to shake ground and get things moving.

What makes me as real as the person holding this book is that, I know how it feels to live paycheck to paycheck. I know what being a single mom by choice is like and how it feels when it isn't by choice. I have been married and divorced with kids, so I can relate to the sore tongue that develops as we 'responsible' parents who bite down, knowing that it's unhealthy to speak badly against the other 'not-so-responsible' parent. I can attest to the power of prayer (both seemingly answered and unanswered). I have ideas as to why things are not forming the way you want them to in your life and a plan to help you light that match. This one little ole' book is more than enough because everyone knows it to be true: You *never* mess with a woman on a mission.

Intro to Grounded in Confidence- is the final part of *From the Ground Up*. I give an introduction to the series of eBooks I developed for seminars and online training environments. I talk briefly about *how, what* and *why* confidence is the foundation of every area in our lives. I also show you how one would use the *Grounded in Confidence Workbook and Journal*. You can follow my series and other similar items on my website at

www.tammyjojohnson.com

Think of this book as "conditioning". In order to prepare for your own big event, you need to be physically, mentally, and emotionally

How to Read This Book

ready. I didn't want to throw you directly into a training environment for confidence without your permission or my story. For some of you, all you really need is a little inspiration and reading about me– here in *From the Ground Up* will give you that. Other may need that extra push—something to get you going and kick your confidence into gear. This light conditioning may be your answer. Lastly, there will be those who have a desire for high self-esteem, but can't get the fire ignited. You have been faced with the fact that you *will probably not* get that promotion based on your talent alone if you have a hard time controlling your emotions. If you do, the first time you are challenged by upper management, you will break down. You have been faced with the possibility that you *will probably not* save your marriage based on seminars and counseling sessions if you're not even sure of what your part is in the demise of it. If you keep trying to change the other person, they will leave you.

Then, there are those of you who *say* you want to be a better spouse, parent, and leader—but you don't even know who you are as an individual. You have never been pushed outside of your own comfort zone nor have you been challenged enough to desire to be. My book, *Grounded in Confidence* along with the workbook will be there for you. So will I.

It's time for a unique learning experience in self-discovery and new found confidence. The feeling of high self-regard has always been in you- it's just hidden.

These ideas and principles stem from years of study, research, trial, error, and results. I've been privileged to so many unique learning environments it was almost like the whole world has been my classroom. In the beginning, I cried, prayed, and screamed to the top of my lungs that I did not want this responsibility. It was too much. I didn't understand how I could help someone else, nor did I have the desire to in the beginning of this journey.

What if my program doesn't work for you? , I used to think.

While I can't promise definite results, I can promise that you will get out of this and any other philosophy what you put into it. What took me almost fifteen years to learn and develop, can equip you in six months or less if you allow it to.

This is not a complicated theory-based thing. It is practical and applicable. It is also very real and attainable to transition into the life you desire. Pulling everything together to make it easy to understand, fun, and do-able was the easy part. I accepted purpose in my past pain. I realized that by taking the lead, disclosing personal information about *my* past for your inspiration and accepting the responsibility that I did not go through *all* of that for "me" was not a burden, but an honor. I am honored that you are even still reading. Most books don't give you real life scenario that you can relate to all the way down to the grammatical errors in the paragraph but the self-publishing and eBook arena is changing that and I get to take part of it.

I also came to know that life never really became real to me until I held a small, helpless life in my arms on June 9, 1999.

My Daughter.

When she entered the world around fourteen years ago, I became dog-determined to not allow any kind of defeated mentality into my surroundings. Nor did I feel like I had a family to care about

How to Read This Book

until she was born. The hardness of my heart, my feelings of entitlement, and all of my selfishness disappeared. My story of overcoming became less about me, and more about her. She became my "why".

I invite you to discover your reason for change and accountability as well. How do you know you are really ready? Ask yourself these three questions and then *DO* something about the answers.

1. Are you tired of wandering this earth knowing you can make a difference but don't know how?

2. Are you tired of trying to meet every standard set by someone else for you and yet still never feel "good enough"?

3. Are you just tired of existing—and don't know why?

Later in the book, we will figure all of that out. But for now, just relax and walk with me into the night that I wish I didn't remember.

Part One – The Story

Chapter One – The Nightmare on My Street

I ran as fast as I could. I felt It behind me getting closer and closer. The hair on the back of my neck stood its peak and I was scared to death.

I couldn't cry.

Crying would've slowed me down.

So I ran. Barefoot, heart pounding violently against my chest, my feet pounded the ground as if my life depended on it. The texture of the ground slowed me down like quicksand and I couldn't run at the speed my mind was trying to communicate to my legs. The desire to not be captured by It made me more determined to press forward losing all consciousness of time.

Time didn't matter. Nothing mattered but getting away from It.

Determination took over logic and I told myself that I would run as long and as far as I needed to in order to survive. I didn't know what It would do to me if It caught me. I imagined horrible pain and torture. I'm not sure why those thoughts bothered me as I was familiar with pain and understood torture. It was hard to reason while I was running for my life.

Forgive me for being rude. I haven't introduced you to the dark, cloudy mass that befriended me in my childhood. A dark, shadow-like presence that didn't carry a physical form yet felt like the strength of a NFL team. *It* appeared fast and out of nowhere like a bolt of lightning.

Every time *It* came around, I felt a sense of overwhelming and intense emotion. *It* was sophisticated in the way *It* shifted and moved. There was nothing familiar enough about *It* to compare *It* to something else. No one ever assisted me with a full description so I always referred to it as "It". Later, when I learned about demonic spirits and the different forms they take on, I felt relieved to know that I was not alone in the spiritual war that is present on this earth.

Some nights, *It* surrounded my bed and hovered over me like a new mother watching her first born preemie. I'd wake-up startled, completely paralyzed and forcefully pinned down to my bed. My mind was alert and I was aware of my surroundings. I could see through my eyes, but just couldn't move. When I struggled to move, a sharp unbearable pain would shoot through my head as if a spear was being jammed into the nerve of my temple. I'd feel like I was falling in and out of consciousness—unsure if I was dreaming, awake, or in a state of un-charted consciousness in between.

I had very few opportunities to escape during these encounters, so, I learned that if I'd relax, my muscles would ease the stronghold and I'd eventually wake up. I don't know why *It* was after *me*, or what I'd done to invite *It* into my life. Like everyone else who seemed to have it for me, *It* was disturbingly loyal and showed no signs of unreliability. So many nights I wanted to fight *It*. I wanted to be brave, bold and take a stand. There was a small, but very distinct voice that told me I could defeat *It* but I never listened to that voice

Chapter One – The Nightmare on My Street

because fighting *It* would've meant facing It… and I never turned around.

Ever.

I felt like I had been running forever, but eventually, distance grew between us. I was back in my room and everything around me came into focus, like an adjustment on a rifle scope. The atmosphere was eerie and cold. I was afraid to make any sudden movements for fear that the chase would begin again. After a little while, I'd drift back off to sleep.

Many nights prior, I'd wake up in a panic, running and screaming that *It* was trying to get me. If I could escape before *It* trapped me, *It* couldn't pin me down. Each night, *It* seemed to get closer and closer to my physical body. I was unable to verbalize, at the time, my irritation, conclusions, and feelings of defeat.

Whatever *It* was and whatever reason *It* chose me is still a mystery. When I think back to this time in my life, along with conclusions from many therapists, It appeared in my life shortly after the molestation and bullying.

My scary dreams were not boogeymen, trolls under the bed, or monsters in the closet. When I would wake up screaming and crying, it was because I had hurt someone else. I was tired of running. What made me the chosen one? Why was it after me? What had I done to attract this leech? These questions penetrated my mind from dusk to dawn on most days. Other nights, were peaceful, except for the night it mattered most.

Dying was an easy decision for me because I really didn't understand what death was. When my puppy died, my mom gave the "reincarnation" talk and Sassy came back to life as Carrot, my pet rabbit. It all made sense to me because in order to wake up from being chased by *It*, I would have to die in my sleep because it was the only way to wake up. In essence, I wasn't concerned with death; I just knew that it would check me out of my current life and offer me a new one.

That's what I wanted- to be someone different, or perhaps an animal. The rebirth of my soul in a new body sounded good to me. My body was worn, disgusting, and tired. A premature death seemed to have been an unmet deadline in my life. Depression, rage, and exhaustion consumed me most of the time. It was creatively covered by good grades and Girl Scouts.

I decided enough was enough.

No more unwanted participation behind closed doors where my cousin wanted to play doctor and put things inside of me, where vomit sometimes came to the rescue. I wasn't stupid; I knew that doctors didn't do those things. I just went along with it because I was told that if I ever said anything, I would get into so much trouble that my mom would send me away. He knew I wouldn't tell because I loved my mom and to upset her to the point of her having to send me away because of causing trouble terrified me.

Who would babysit my nephew and niece if she had errands to run?

Who would she have to help take care of things when my half-brothers were gone?

On that night, the fear of my absence was no longer enough to keep me from my death. I wanted to die in reality because when I died in my dreams, I woke up in the same life with the same body. I

Chapter One – The Nightmare on My Street

tried to die so many times that I was beginning to wonder if I was even good enough for death.

The way I understood my life is that I was an accident. I was born and I created this harmonious orchestra of chaotic destruction that caused people to repeatedly afflict pain and suffering simply by existing.

I was born.

I was the cause of the discord among my family when I mentioned that my cousin touched my private area in the backseat of my mom's car.

I was born.

I created the strife that caused my brothers to be in jail which forced my mom to take custody of my nephew which caused unforeseen hardship and drama on all of us. The uproar that swept through the middle school with police officers and concerned parents after blowing the whistle on my friend's brother after he tried to force himself on me was caused by me.

I was also the reason why the milk spilled in the refrigerator, the eggs were broken in the carton, the dog died in the back yard, the real reason why my mom had to pay Christian school tuition and why darkness pursued me– yet never got closer than a breath away from my skin. I felt like a disease that infected everyone who came in my presence.

I was born. But why did I have to suffer? I never asked to be.

To die that night didn't seem like a bad idea to me. I had dreamt about it after I watched it on television in a movie on HBO. I had it all wrong and thought maybe *that* was the issue. I would jump off buildings, step in front of cars, dive off of bridges and jump out of planes. I never thought about a gun because I never encountered one in my dream while on the run. One shot to my brain would've ended everything. Then, I could start life new as someone or something else.

My funeral may have caused a few tears, struck up a conversation in the community for a period of time, then back to life as usual. No one would really miss me. I, on the other hand would have a new start.

No more running.

No more fear.

No more being the cause of evil in innocent people to make them hurt me or any other kids in the family. I wanted to protect them. In order to protect them, I needed to get rid of me.

Jesus died for other people's sins, I was taught earlier that week in a hot church gymnasium. Everyone seemed to love Him *after* he was gone and His mission was complete. I wanted the same. I wanted to matter without being present and be remembered as the hero who made it happen.

A few nights prior, I had a gun in my dream and tried to shoot myself in the head. When I woke up and knew I was awake, I wasn't afraid, I was mad. I was mad because it didn't do anything differently than my other attempts did. What did it really mean to die if dying only meant waking up into the same life? I attempted to tell my mom once that her logic about old souls in new bodies

Chapter One – The Nightmare on My Street

was bullshit. I remember screaming at her, "But I died". She'd rock me back and forth and say, "No baby, you just had a bad dream".

No one understood. Not even her.

According to the therapist my mom tried to drag me to, I suffered from dissociative identity and dream anxiety disorder, but to me, it was warfare; I'd fight to wake up, I'd fight for my life and I'd fight for the right to breathe the air that *It* blocked every time when *It* pinned me to my bed.

I didn't talk to those doctors. I wasn't impressed by the ink blots, kinetic sculptures and pendulums. The couches were way too big, didn't match the color scheme and the office was lit like the home of a vampire. They seemed uncaring and more concerned with the clock on the wall. The time I wasted by refusing to utter a word was filled in with the conversation they carried on with my mom. She didn't seem to mind that they scribbled more than they listened to what she said.

If it wasn't for my mom's rule to respect all elders, I would've told them where to shove their pens. I would've also told them to write on their yellow, legal sized paper that regardless of what they named *It*, fed *It*, and studied *It*, *It* would never go away–unless I went away.

The objective of death became personal, even obsessive.

My mom listened intently to what those doctors were saying, but she never listened intently to me. I'm not talking about verbally taking in information, because I didn't offer her any to listen to and *that's* what I wanted her to hear.

I became fixed on figuring out how to die as if my life depended on it. I would show them that I didn't have to live this life if I didn't want to. I didn't have to stick around and continue to let people do whatever they wanted to me. I wanted my mom to personally carry my lifeless body away and bury it so deep into the ground that no one would remember it. I wanted the dirt pile that covered my casket to conceal whatever attracted the evil presence that I was forced to surrender to. I wanted to finally introduce her to the war going on inside of me that took form in my subconscious.

My one attempt to reveal this battle failed, so all I could do was cry. Her reaction was to pad the wall corners of the house, triple lock the doors and sleep on the couch. She feared my nightly sprinting jolts would cause me physical harm. Nothing on earth could cause me more harm than the slow destruction of my soul. I knew it and so did everyone else;

I was broken beyond repair and my decision was made.

Self-destruction was my destination that night. My cross too was heavy and I wanted Heaven way more than I wanted to go to the 8th grade. This was it. It was now my time to be heard. I had been ruined. Stripped. I felt crucified. To be non-existent, yet fully understood was what I desired. To make them feel bad. Sorry for what they did to me.

Tonight was the night that I would no longer be succumbing to fear or pain. Tonight, I would run no more.

Feel no more.

Be no more.

'I remembered seeing a gun under my mom's mattress a few months back. I came across it on accident when I was cleaning her room as

Chapter One – The Nightmare on My Street

a surprise for her. She never slept in her room anymore because of my nightmare issues and therefore her bedroom became a dumping ground for clothes, mail and shoes. I figured if I made her bed look nice, she'd want to sleep in it again. My mom had back problems from her job which I assumed sleeping on the couch didn't make better. When I went to lift her mattress, there it was along with an enormous amount of papers.

I wondered who it belonged to or why she needed it. I never touched it, it scared me. Ironically, I had never given it any more thought until that night. I went to her room and lifted the mattress at the corner where I'd found it before.

It disappeared.

I became irritated and upset.

As soon as my mom left the house, I impatiently searched everywhere for it. I looked in drawers, under drawers and in boxes in her closet. I looked through empty suitcases and purses, shoe boxes and bags. I tore my mom's room up and I knew that I needed to clean it back up before she got home. By the time I got done cleaning, I was so physically and mentally exhausted that I forgot I was looking for something.

A couple of nights later, I woke up from a dream where I tortured and beat my cousin with a stick for trying to put himself inside of me.

In real life, he tried once but he couldn't. The pain was so intense that I screamed and bit him. He never tried to do that again, but I paid the price for biting him. He stuck his fingers inside of me while forcing me to suck on him. I was crying so hard that I couldn't do it the way she showed me and when I didn't he'd shove his finger inside my vagina. I couldn't make myself vomit because I was too angry and was in too much pain. I beg and pleaded for him to stop and he told me he would when he was done. I guess the pain he was causing between my legs signaled a boiling point in my tolerance because I was mad. I was so mad that I bit down on him as hard as I could and ran screaming and crying from the room. I called my mom to come get me. When she asked me what was wrong and why was I crying, my cousin had already picked up the landline in the other room and told her I had a nightmare. I didn't see my cousin no more after that which is why this dream seemed necessary.

I was beating him with a stick. He was bleeding out of his ear and onto the concrete of the playground of my elementary school. I tied his hands and feet up with jump rope. In the dream it was day time. No one was on the playground, but him and me. I stuffed his mouth with grass while kicking him and beating him with the stick. I pulled down his pants and crammed the stick between his legs. He started to laugh. My dream shifted to nighttime and It *showed up as it always had. In my dreams where* It *appeared meant that something really bad was going to happen. In order for* It *not to chase me, I had to allow* It *to help me. When* It *helped me, I was afraid because* It *always did something ten times worse than I'd wanted to.*

I remember the fear in my cousin's eyes when It *appeared. He was no longer laughing, he was afraid. To watch the fear in his eyes like that gave me permission to let him have whatever was coming to him.*

My hand was full of fire. It was a blue and orange fire that was so bright, it lit up the entire playground. I was about to set my cousin on fire when out the corner of my eye, I saw a little boy running towards me from the swings. He was screaming "No, don't hurt him!." It *forced me*

Chapter One – The Nightmare on My Street

to throw the fire in the direction of the little boy, but before it reached him, he screamed "No! Auntie!"

I watched the little boy burst into flames and I woke up.

When I awakened, I was already in my mom's arms rocking back and forth screaming and crying as I had been so many times. It felt as if my soul was taken away from my body and then put back in my body when I woke up. When I woke up in my mom's arms, I instantly felt the physical exhaustion and intensity in my body. It was like I had been there crying and screaming long before the dream was even over. But once I was aware that I was awake, I could calm myself down.

Once I was calm enough to convince my mom that I was ok, she went back to the couch and lay down. That night, I was far from ok. I wept for what seemed like hours. I was afraid to go back to sleep.

I loved my nephew more than anything in my life at that time. He was like my baby and I took care of him. He was three. During that summer, we'd convinced him to be a big boy and sleep in the spare bedroom with my younger cousin who was there for the summer. My mom created the spare bedroom for that reason. My nephew liked my younger cousin because he was a little boy too and he didn't get to be around little boys that much. They played together and kept busy while I did the dishes most of the time.

My nephew had been through so much with his mom not having custody of him and my brother being locked away that I vowed to take care of him until one or both parents came to their senses. I didn't know enough about what was going on to judge either one of them. What I did know is that with my mom and I, my nephew was safe and cared for.

The dream disturbed something in my heart. I got up and went to the bathroom to wash my face. I looked like crap. My eyes were swollen beyond recognition and my hair was a wild mess. I really was ugly, just like the kids at school said. I went to the spare bedroom to check on my nephew. I knew that it was just a dream, but I wanted him to be close to me because something told me that *It* was no longer just after me. I opened the door quietly so that I wouldn't wake up my younger cousin too because then he would want to come too and both of them plus me would not get any sleep in my twin bed. My nephew's comforter was too heavy for me to try to carry him and it to my room, so I figured a sheet would be lighter and easier. I quietly opened the closet and began searching for a twin sheet and that's where I saw it. When I saw the black winter skully hat in between the two boxes on the shelf, it thought it strange to be there in July. When I grabbed it, I immediately knew what was hidden inside.

My sadness slowly subsided.

I quietly and carefully picked it up and took it to my room. When I took it out of the hat it was in a case. It was smaller than I remembered and felt surprisingly heavy. I thought that if I took it out of the case it would go off but fear was not the dominating feeling. I took it out the case and held it carefully. It created feelings in me that I had never felt before.

Power.

Peace.

Chapter One – The Nightmare on My Street

Closure.

I placed it under my pillow, laid down, and the thoughts began to race:

Could it really wipe away my current existence with just pulling the trigger? I thought only God had that type of power. Would I get in trouble? What if my mom tried to take it from me? Would it hurt or would I feel anything or would I just be immediately transferred to another life? When I die will I go to that Heaven they talked about at church? Or would God be furious with me for trying to re-do my life on my own and send me through hell first? Or …was I dreaming all of this?

I slid my hand under my pillow to make sure the gun was there. The thoughts continued:

It didn't matter; no one really cared what happened to me. Maybe my niece, nephew and cousin would miss me—but they had mom. They would always have her. With me out of the way, they would be safe and It *would go away. I'd be doing them a favor by dying. It was strangely quiet that night. My thoughts were louder than usual but I felt no fear because I knew that dying meant waking up and whatever nightmare found me, it was time to end it. If reincarnation was wrong or heaven and hell didn't really exist, I knew I would just wake up like I did plenty of times when I jumped off a building or dived off the bridge in order to wake up.*

This is where things got confusing.

I was no longer sleepy. In fact, I thought it was almost time to get up, but apparently the thoughts got so heavy that I rested. This rest wasn't interrupted, not even a little. That one moment when I felt myself waking up, I sprang up to sitting position on my bed. The thought that I fell asleep after what I dreamt terrorized me.

What time was it? Where was my nephew? I thought I brought him in the room with me?

The night's activities came back to me.

The gun! I had a gun!

I felt under my pillow and the gun was there. I was relieved and immediately pulled it from under the pillow and took it out of its case.

It was now or never. If I put the gun back, I may not be able to find it again.

I knew what I had to do.

The atmosphere was strange yet familiar. *It* was here, I could feel *It* by the way the air got cold. I knew that there was no turning back now because once *It* arrived I have two choices: to comply, or to run. *It* seemed to know what my plan was and wanted to be around to see through to fruition.

I didn't want to be alone in my room when I died. There were feelings of wanting my mom to find me dead. I took the gun and walked to the living room. It was dark and the only light in the room was the clock with large bright blue numbers, except they used to be red.

I didn't give it too much thought.

I put the gun up to the side of my head and pulled the trigger with no hesitation. The clicking sound of the unexpected empty chamber crossed paths with the familiar surroundings of my nightmare,

Chapter One – The Nightmare on My Street

which interrupted my intent. I wasn't sure if I was dreaming, awake, or dead. From that moment on everything intensified and felt like the speed of light. I felt *Its* cold presence.

It *had come back for me!*

It hovered over the couch in front of the window before *It* bolted towards me. I shot at *It* multiple times hearing clicking noises before realizing the gun didn't work, I dropped it and ran out of the house screaming.

I ran just as I had many times before, not looking back. I was almost two blocks before I realized *It* was no longer behind me. I felt tired and cold and was still alive, but I knew in order for this nightmare to end someone had to die. Then, I remembered the dream about my nephew.

The clock was supposed to be red! Not blue! The fire in my hand was blue before it forced me to throw it at my nephew!

I ran back towards the house screaming for help at the top of my lungs,

"It's going to shoot fire! It's going to shoot fire at my mom! Somebody help me!"

I knew my mom was in trouble because she was the only other person in the dream. I never brought my nephew in the room with me because I got distracted when I found the gun.

No one could help me, this was my fight, and I was the only one who could stop It.

Someone grabbed me right before I reached the front yard. I was crying and screaming and trying to explain that I had to get inside of the house so I could stop *It* from setting my mom on fire. Whoever had me, held me tight. I heard someone say,

"She's been shot."

Flashes of lights covered the street; people were crying and hugging me.

The dream was no longer a familiar one.

People in my dreams didn't cry and no one was dead, because I wasn't awake yet.

Confusion hit me hard; I stopped processing. Everything after that went pitch black and apparently, *that* method of self-soothing was not ok.

I was admitted to a special room on the psychiatric floor of Children's Hospital.

I only remember the smell of band aids and graham crackers. I remember white coats and what my room looked like. From the reports I read and gathering what information I could from family, I was released a week later and was diagnosed with Post Traumatic Stress Disorder (PTSD).

Chapter Two – Handle the Truth with Care

I was sent home with relatives. When people asked me what happened that night, I told them I didn't know. When I heard other people talking about it, I began to repeat what they were saying. I would ask,

"When is my mom coming to get me?"

No one ever answered me. I learned of one report that said a neighbor saw someone running from the house and another said that someone was trying to rob us. I held on to their story and allowed it to settle in me because I didn't have one. All I knew was as soon as my mom came for me, everything would be ok. But she never came, and I didn't understand why.

After the visit at the hospital, I declared I would never think about that nightmare again. Another part of me fought against that declaration. Something didn't connect and there was a new war going on inside of me. I was around family and life seemed to be normal but two things seemed to be suddenly misplaced; my mom and my nephew. I couldn't fight the thoughts any longer.

Something is wrong. Where are they and why is no one is telling me anything?

I felt like part of me was protecting me from another part of me. I did talk to police and detectives. I remember them swabbing my hands at the police station. At the time, I didn't know that someone had died or that I was a suspect. There was no way for me to describe to them at twelve what I am telling you now. In my mind I had another nightmare. My guess is, if they did ask me questions, I just regurgitated what I heard everyone else saying. My hands were clean so they sent me home.

Other relatives took me to the beach, I assumed, to take my mind off of things. I was actually laughing and having a good time. I met a boy I liked and I remember how peaceful the water looked on the horizon. I felt that the water was somehow involved. I was mesmerized by it and wanted to walk out to the deeper part because I felt like something was calling to me, something stronger as the water got deeper. The splashing and laughing distracted me during the time we were at the beach, but as soon as I stood still, my mind raced. The thoughts turned into questions and got louder.

Why was I in the hospital in the first place? I wasn't hurt. Why did that nightmare not end like the other ones? Why did it seem like my life was somehow different? Why is everyone so nice to me all of a sudden? Where are my mom and my nephew?

I tried really hard not to think about the nightmare that was different, but so many questions kept coming to the front of my mind and every time they did, it was like something on the inside of my brain would knock it out of the way and force me to think of something else. That would happen every time I stood still or was left alone.

Chapter Two – Handle the Truth with Care

When I think back, I alone probably would've never been able to ask myself the questions that really mattered. Like, is that gun still under my pillow? Or, where is my mom and nephew, did *It* get them and take them away?

It took the audible voice of someone else to break that protection in my mind. Of course I didn't understand that then, but while reading about me and learning about what the doctors said went on in my mind it all seemed to make sense. There was a part of me that knew that there was a relationship between my dream about my nephew, my dream about the neighbors not letting me in the house, the fact that I shot a gun that didn't work and the disappearance of my mom and nephew.

My uncle took me for a walk some days later. I knew the walk had a purpose and I felt prepared for it even though I didn't know what would unfold. He was the dad of my younger cousin that was with us that summer and my mom's younger brother. He didn't come around often, but when he did I knew him. He was a male authority in my life and my mom loved him. He lived with us for a short time, but I don't remember too much detail. I do remember that if he ever heard me mouth off to my mom all he had to do was turn and look my way and I'd straighten up– quickly.

As I got older and looked back on that day he took me for a walk, I understood why. It made sense that it was him who asked the question that cocooned itself deep into the inner parts of my conscious. The one question that I hid from myself and dared not ask. He was the owner of the gun.

"What really happened that night?", he asked.

That question echoed into my eardrum, travelled into my throat and pierced through whatever barrier was protecting me from having that conversation with myself. That wall was destroyed. It all came rushing to me as if I was being thrown into another realm. My mind remembered bits and pieces and the pieces that were missing were substituted and quickly analyzed with logic from my own imagination. I didn't know whether to talk about what was chasing me or what I had planned to do. Because I still was unsure about what was real and what was dream. The pit of my stomach churned and it felt as if I regurgitated a mass so heavy that my insides erupted.

I don't know if it ever verbalized into an audible sentence or if the thought of it that caused my crying gave it away. I will never forget the answer that changed the course of my entire life,

"I think I shot Mom". My uncle held me as I poured out what I felt was the last bit of mental and emotional energy I had left. My mind began to create pictures that only existed because of imagination, along with pictures I didn't remember. The thoughts I did remember, I doubted, because of my dreams. I thought that from there, my uncle was going to take me to see my mom. I thought that maybe the gun did go off and I had just awakened into another nightmare. This was not uncommon. At that age, I marched in a band, I played sports, and I was badge-earning Girl Scout. I knew nothing about crime, jail, murder, or death for that matter.

My mind was too unsettled and immature to articulate and verbalize factual information that would satisfy a police statement. When I was told my finger prints came back clear, I really lacked clarification and understanding of what took place, but I tried very hard

Chapter Two – Handle the Truth with Care

to offer pieces of what I did. Trying to explain my dreams out loud always ended in confusion and frustration.

My prior experience taught me that no one would understand. I later found out that understanding was secondary.

I was placed in the local detention center for nine months until my sentence hearing. I did not have a trial because I admitted to firing the gun. After the first month in that place a male correctional officer sexually molested me and convinced me that if I told anyone, things would be worse for me. *That* sounded familiar and who was I to argue? Not only had I hurt someone else, I figured my body was no longer any good anyway from all the disgusting things my cousin had done to it. I deserved anything that inflicted pain, especially if I really did what they accused me of, so I let him have his way.

I was forced to talk to pro-bono lawyers, prosecutors, psychologist, social workers and other juveniles who verbalized their own version of what happened. The interrogations caused the visual sequences to keep changing in my mind. That caused an irritating inability to make sense of it all. I assume that's where dissociation created a safe haven for my mind.

The conclusion I drew later during my investigations, is that the phrases:

"Gun under pillow",

"Nightmare",

"Suicide" and

"Running from *It*"

from a thirteen year old was enough for the charge "aggravated murder by reason of temporary insanity".

I was sentenced to a juvenile correctional facility until the age of twenty-one. The length of time that was didn't really sink in until later. I don't believe I was processing any information on a deep level.

When I first arrived, there was a sign that read "Scioto School for Girls". It looked like a youth camp. It sat on a large, green acre land space with large and small cottage like cabin homes. The group leaders wore blue and there were hundreds of girls in pink, red and green shirts. Everyone I came in contact with seemed friendly. I felt safe.

The atmosphere alone reminded me of being a Girl Scout. Our troop would participate in five-day camping trips away from home. While I was away from home, I couldn't be bullied or molested. I canoed, climbed walls, hiked, sang around a campfire, and burned marshmallows. Life as a Girl Scout was a fun part of my life, so I lived in that state of mind for a long time. I was too far away from home for anyone to hurt me.

As the years inside of the institution passed, juvenile crime increased. The camp-like atmosphere was slowly replaced by a correctional institution. The name changed to

"Scioto Juvenile Correctional Facility".

Acres of green grass were interrupted by barbed-wire fences and gone were the log cabin cottages with bunk beds, game rooms and kitchens. Brick walls with small windows, matching uniforms and

Chapter Two – Handle the Truth with Care

heavy metal doors with steel locks that clicked loudly when closed was now the place I'd called home until I was twenty one years old.

No matter how many times the word "*murder*" or "*death*" circulated in my presence while getting used to the facility,

I accepted neither.

I understood neither.

I secretly waited for my mom to show up at the institution for a long time. I assumed that she would come and clear things up as she did at my school or with my coaches even if I was wrong. I knew that I would eventually wake up from this nightmare.

Neither ever happened.

I didn't fully understand for quite a while that taking someone's life meant that they would never return. I didn't receive the fact that I could no longer make a nightmare go away by self sacrifice and that waking up was no longer an option.

The realization of what I'd done hit the center nerve of my heart. I was around fifteen when I began to comprehend that my original plan was hijacked and I would never see my mom again.

I was no longer an A-student, baton-twirling, cheerleading Girl Scout, I was a murderer.

And I didn't know what to do with that.

Chapter Three – My Life. My View.

I have been victimized.

I was in a fight that was not a fair fight.

I did not ask for the fight.

I lost.

There is no shame in losing such fights.

I have reached the stage of survivor and am no longer a slave of victim status.

I look back with sadness rather than hate.

I look forward with hope rather than despair.

I may never forget, but I need not constantly remember.

I WAS a victim.

I AM a survivor.

– Poem by Frank Ochberg from the book "Gift From Within"-

Akron was all I'd ever known. I was born there. As a little girl to a single mom in a middle class neighborhood, walking to school, to the store or riding bikes around the neighborhood is what we did on a daily basis. I never knew my dad because he died when I was three years old on his job site. I met my sister (my dad's daughter) years later and learned a lot about that side of the family. Meeting and getting to know my sister as an adult continues to teach me what I didn't realize long ago, but would've helped to know, is that I wasn't alone.

I had two older half-brothers, but only saw them on and off. They were in and out of the penitentiary for drug abuse. I'm not sure if it's suppressed memory or if they weren't around enough for me to have any real memory of them but the one thing I remember about my brother Drew is that he loved music. When he did come home, his funk and rock music drove my mom crazy. When he would leave again, I'd find his records and eight tracks and listen to them in my room.

My other brother MJ was different. The only thing I remember about him is that he called me "Tam". People always used to say that I favor him, but when I would look up his picture it was usually a mug shot and who wants to resemble that?

Sometimes while they were gone, I would be mad at them for not being around to protect me. I never gave expression to that frustration and it didn't last because when they came around it was always fun. When they didn't come around for a while and I saw my mom pack boxes of spam, white socks and underwear, I knew that we wouldn't see them for quite some time.

My mom and I were close. She was a single mom and never brought strange men around the house. It was just me, her, and my nephew.

Chapter Three – My Life. My View.

She was an amazing woman. She was the glue that held everything and everyone together. Her wisdom and creativity was the reason people called on her when there was a wedding, or other special occasion. She had a special ability to bring everything and everyone together-seamlessly. They received her instruction with no hesitation.

The clothes that the kids at school gave me a hard time for wearing were designed and made by her. Her state-of-the-art sewing machine was always on and ready to create or repair. I was proud and wore them with pride.

She was also a pre-teen's nightmare. I couldn't do anything I wanted when I wanted to. I wasn't permitted to roam the streets like most of my peers. I was held to a pretty tight rope. Sometimes it seemed too tough and the tears seemed endless, other times I appreciated her because she protected me the best way she knew how. I may have been a brat to a lot of people because she spoiled me rotten, but I was also made to respect my elders, clean my room, do the dishes, and have a phone-only boyfriend. Sometimes, she'd call me from all the way outside to come in the house and give her the television remote–priceless. She thought she was checking on me. I thought she was being unreasonable.

Until years later when I had my daughter.

My mom was crazy about me. She fussed over me and bought me things anytime she was away from the house. My schedule stayed busy as a majorette, cheerleader, and Girl Scout and she always asked how school was going and stayed on top of my grades. I wasn't allowed to bring home average, because to her, I was far from it. She rewarded me for babysitting my nephew when she had to make runs so I always looked forward to it. He was like a live baby doll that I got to feed, change, and love. I was crazy about him.

I read a lot of books, listened to all kinds of music, and got into trouble when I broke the rules. I was praised for my accomplishments and disciplined for disobedience.

I was loved.

Revealing anything to my mom that was outside the realm of the happiness she worked so hard to create would disappoint her. I didn't want to be a disappointment. My nightmare attacks, her fighting to keep custody of my nephew, and caring for my two older half-brothers in prison were enough and it wore on her. I wasn't too young to understand that.

Life with my mom appeared simple and normal to everyone else.

That's how I wanted to keep it.

Chapter Four – Bullied and Taunted

I had everything a girl could want.

Except peace.

I was bullied from around the 4th through 8th grade. I was timid and quiet in nature. I was likeable by mostly white kids even though I had darker skin and was often referred to as "blackie" or "tar-face" by the black kids. I wore red framed glasses that held a strong prescription which made my eyes small and my glasses unfashionable. Other kids called me "pop bottle eyes", "four-eyes" or my favorite "Sally Jessie Raphael". I had very few friends to call my own, but there were a few. The name calling didn't bother me much that I knew of and I grew accustomed to it.

My fashion sense was appalling because most of the time the clothes that the other kids wore, we couldn't afford. I was so excited when she finally made me the MC Hammer pants I saw in the store, they were my favorite—I wore them a lot. I was also the girl who wore the jean skirt with the ruffles and tennis shoes. I also wore a lot of my mom's clothes because they were baggy on me. They covered me in a way that I felt protected me from people touching me.

My body frame was structured to where my butt appeared bigger than what it was and it took up residence on my back which forced me to walk like a duck. Family and peers made fun of me because of the way I walked.

I was dubbed the ugly duckling. I felt that way every day that I woke up and went to school.

There was a girl in my school who over towered me by about two feet. I only saw her in the school building a couple of times throughout the day. Her and her friends would bump into me in the hall and call after me with one of my many "nicknames". Nothing I wore ever met their approval and my hair was too thick and "nappy", they called it. I don't recall having an actual argument with her, but by the time the bell rang for recess almost every day, she was in my face accusing me of something. The accusations were always false and I finally came to the conclusion that it didn't matter, I was her outlet. I don't even recall having any classes with her.

She'd get in my face, say a few choice words and told me why she was going to "beat my ass" and would then proceed to do just that —consistently. I got to a point where I'd rather her hit me than call me names and poke fun of my clothes. When she talked about me she invited others to have an opinion, but when she began to hit me, no one else ever did. I guess they figured I was doing a pretty good job getting my ass kicked on my own.

Teachers would look the other way. They saw what was going on but they never said anything. I remember one teacher Ms. Dowey, actually walked right past a crowd in the hallway. She was a nice looking, tall black woman and mean. I heard stories about her and was so relieved that I never had to sit in a class where she taught.

Chapter Four – Bullied and Taunted

As she started walking toward us, I figured she'd jump in—but she didn't. She walked right pass as if we were exchanging greeting cards and gummy bears. I lost respect for her as a teacher.

As soon as most teachers were out of sight, my nemesis would punch me right in the face. My glasses were scratched and broken so often that I eventually had to tape them together. The only tape that seemed to do the trick was black tape. My mom would always yell at me for not wearing them. I finally pulled them out and showed her the damage. I'd told her I dropped them and tried to put them back together so she wouldn't have to buy me another pair.

After lecturing me about being responsible and the purpose for the case, she bought me another pair. I was relieved because at least the new pair came with a black frame.

The bullying was random and often but the fights were few. I tried to fight back physically, the best I knew how. I never said much or trash talked. I had to focus on how not to get hit. I needed any advantage I could get. When I got suspended from school for fighting, it appeared as if the platform was even. My mom was proud of me for defending myself at least and I received a three day break from hell. Her philosophy was if I got beat up at school, I would get beat up when I got home—by her. "You can't let people beat on you because they won't stop". She was right about that, but I obviously needed a plan B.

When I arrived home, suspension papers in hand, her only question and concern was, "did you win?" Needless to say, I had mastered the art of storytelling by my final year in elementary.

There were things going on at home that made me look forward to going to school. I spent most of my time babysitting. I loved my niece and nephew so much because they were babies to me. I mothered them like my mom did me. I protected them like my mom did

me. I also played with them. There were no electronics or handheld game systems and the internet didn't exist. We had an Atari, Barbie dolls, Easy Bake Oven, play kitchen sets, utensils and elements of the earth. When I played with them or the two other little girls in my neighborhood, I was a kid. Then I remembered that my body didn't feel like it was.

Living outside of the pain that was brewing inside of me was so easy. It came so natural to pretend to be the girl everyone expected me to be. As long as I got the grades, made the team, or babysat the kids, life was well.

Most of the kids in our family flocked over to our house. They always came over in sets and never wanted to leave. My two closest cousins, Meech and Dom, were there the most fun to be around and when they came over adventure was always promised. They were the children of my maternal grandmothers' sister's daughter's kids (phew!). We would go deep into the woods in the back of my house and get lost for hours. We learned about the railroad tracks and a cliff that ended the wood trail and often played warrior with sticks and abandoned car parts. We climbed trees, made mud wagons, and tortured each other like brothers. We summer camped together, fought over turns when we played Pac-Man and Frogger until my mom took the joy sticks. We'd make up with a spit handshake and all was well with our world. This is when I was my true happy tom-boy self. I didn't like the color pink, I hated anything with lace and the pumps my mom tried to get me to wear to school

Chapter Four – Bullied and Taunted

were replaced before the first bell by my dirty, smelly L.A. Gears that I hid in my bag.

Other relative visits weren't so pleasant. My older distant cousins decided to use me as a sexual party favor. They would take turns and make me do explicit things to make them feel good. They said that if I ever said anything, I would be seen as a trouble maker, get taken away from my mom, and that no one would believe me. They were good at manipulation and I felt like I needed to protect my niece and nephew from them. They depended on me and looked for me to protect them. Having them around was a joy for me because I felt needed. It angered me to imagine what my older cousins would do to them, if I weren't around. So I did whatever they wanted.

I decided to keep those secrets hidden away. I had sense enough to know what causes uproars in families and I didn't want to be a target. I was afraid that if other people in the family knew what they were doing to me, then others would try and do the same thing. Safety and protection did not feel like a part of my reality.

Deep inside of me, I grew hatred toward those who hurt me. On the surface, I could smile, laugh, and play scrabble, but the girl who did that seemed like a separate person. I remember what that felt like. What I didn't understand at the time is how my "assertive girl" self was able to protect "the sad girl" self without me giving direction.

When my cousins were not molesting me, I didn't feel the physical pain from them. The pain I felt was more achy and distorted. I hated what they were doing, but when they were not doing it, I felt sorry for what I did to them in my dreams because when I would dream, I really felt like I was hurting them. When I went to sleep at night, I would have nightmares torturing them like they did me. I didn't like the nightmares because to me it was real and I didn't know it wasn't real until I woke up. I felt like something was wrong with *me* for them to do the things they did.

I never wondered if they were hurting someone else. I didn't even see it as wrong because it became a part of my norm and all I had to do was master the art of secrecy in order to keep this life the way it had always been. Mine.

Dysfunctional and appreciated.

Chapter Five – Dream Anxiety Disorder

My nightmares started to become day problems. Most nights when I closed my eyes something dark surrounded me. It turned me evil and put me in a world where I killed the people who were hurting me. While I was hurting them, I never felt remorse or showed mercy until I woke up and realized it was a nightmare. When I didn't wake up running from It, I woke up crying because I thought I hurt someone. In my night world, I was an avenger, but the evil kind. I tortured my bullies, carved eyeballs out of my cousins, and left them bleeding, crying and pleading for their life. After I tortured them, the demon-like figure that I refer to as "It", would chase me until I killed myself in my dream. That was the only way to know for sure that I was dreaming and the only way to wake myself up. Sometimes, I would think that I was awake and actually be inside of another dream. This confused me all the time.

Unfortunately, the characters in my nightmares didn't like secrets or bullies. Both paid for what they were doing to me in my subconscious. I was both powerful and afraid of *that* version of me.

My mom asked me one day if anyone else was picking on me at school and I decided to spill the beans. She was heated. The look on her face along with a few choice words confused me as to whom she was angry at. She reassured me that it wasn't me.

As any parent would, my mom called a conference with the teacher and administration. They were not helpful or supportive. In fact, they asked her if she was certain, that I wasn't the bully. When she realized she wasn't going to get anywhere with them, she begged and pleaded with me to fight back. She felt what any parent in her shoes would feel:

Helpless.

Eventually, my mom called out to the avenger that lurked in my soul without realizing it. It was fall and I borrowed her new white jogging suit that she told me I couldn't wear because it was too big. I figured out a way to fold over the pants and wore a t-shirt underneath the sweatshirt. I had no idea what was coming that day.

I guess I should've listened because that day, I had a really hard time keeping my clothes from falling and sliding. I was in study hall and received a pass to go to the bathroom. It was toward the end of the day and I knew that band class was my last period. I also knew that I had to change back into the clothes that I left the house in so that I wouldn't get into trouble. Because it was almost time for the bell to ring for band class, I decided to take a detour to the lower level of the school so I could change. I was ashamed of my body, so I didn't want to change in the bathroom where anyone could see. I headed toward the vacant classroom by the band room.

I ran into Trey. I knew of him, but never really had a conversation with him. He was in the eighth grade and stood about 6ft. I don't recall a long conversation, but he wouldn't let me get to where I was

Chapter Five – Dream Anxiety Disorder

going. He mumbled something about me having sex with him. He said "I know you like me". At first, I thought he was just playing around but I soon found out otherwise. He didn't get to do much damage because I was already that. I was telling him to stop, but he wouldn't.

I was sexually assaulted during school hours.

The "avenger me" that I was afraid of during my nightmares refused to be held captive to the subconscious mind any longer. Likewise, there is a line in every mom that you dare not cross for fear of the unknown. When I went to the school office who called the police then my mom, that line was crossed.

I was examined, he was convicted. I refused counseling because I felt in control of my feelings and I decided that after a few days, I was going back to school. I didn't care about what happened to my body, I was just pissed about being forced to do something with another person that I didn't want to do. In my eyes, he ruined my day. In my mom's eyes, he ruined my life.

She was so angry that another family member had to calm her down. I never saw my mom like that. It placed a responsibility in my mind to make things go away. I figured if I did that, life would go back to normal.

When I got back to school, I was surrounded by whispers and stares. To some, I was a whore and to others I was a victim. Even though he wasn't charged with "rape" because I struggled enough not to let him penetrate me, it didn't take long for the peanut gallery to surface. I was either a whore for allowing it, or a bitch for telling; therefore I was loved by even less and hated by even more.

This one boy wanted to fight me after school a few days later. The telegram didn't come from the opponent, it came by messenger. Unfortunately, in middle school, it doesn't matter who the message came from, it was tried and true. I had an appointment at three-o-clock on the next school day. I don't remember if him wanting to fight me had anything to do with the rumors. In middle school though, no excuse was needed.

I was afraid. I broke down in tears and told my mom everything that had been happening at school.

By this time, I was not only ill-equipped to fight a boy, I was tired.

Tired of the secrets.

Tired of the pain.

Just plain tired.

For the first time ever, my mom sat me down and spoke through me directly into my soul. She talked with me other times before, but that conversation felt different. It was the consistency of her tears, the tone in her voice and the love in her heart. The information became too much for me to listen, but the "other me", was all ears. I didn't want to hear about hurting someone; I did that all night long while I slept. I remember being torn by two afflicting feelings.

"Look, you are going to have to prove that you are not a punching bag. I can't do this for you, only you can. You're going to have to hurt someone in order to be heard. Once you take out the toughest one in the crowd all the others will back off. You're going to have to trust me on this," she said.

As she spoke to me, I remember the boiling irritation swelling and arising in me and the power that was familiar to my dreams. The

Chapter Five – Dream Anxiety Disorder

"avenger me" that tortured and fought in my dreams was being called out. I also remember feeling very afraid. I wasn't afraid for my life, I was afraid for his. Tears filled my eyes as if I was going on the battlefield of life. They weren't tears of fear or anxiety. They were tears of anger and rage.

I was so caught up in my thoughts; I never noticed the two sharpened pencils she placed in my hand. Evil and revenge come front and center to my body and pushed the weak sad me to the back end. I stopped feeling angry and began to feel powerful. My mom nodded at me as if she understood what I was feeling and said,

"If someone…anyone, invades your space, you stab them and you don't let up until they are on the ground bleeding or dead. I can't give you a knife, or I would. Defend yourself now and never worry again. Let someone else hurt you and you will have to deal with me."

I nodded in agreement. My mom's directive was clear; all hell—no mercy. My objective was also clear; I was to fight– not only him who called me out, but to show them *all* that I would no longer be a sexual pleasure filled punching bag. To fight back no matter what. This fight wasn't just to defend myself from the boy who called me out. In my mind, this fight was just the beginning of my war with anyone who dared to hurt me again.

I was ready. I checked on my pencils though out the day and could hardly wait until after school. I couldn't concentrate. The boy that called the battle wasn't even in the forefront of my mind. The bullies before him, my cousins, and anybody who *thought* about hurting me would pay on that day. Stabbing him would send a message to everyone else were words would no longer be required.

The bell rang. The ringing of the bell both altered and startled me. Based on what I was told by therapists, that is when my dissociative disorder became the most obvious. They explained that the personality who was timid and afraid was pushed out of the way and the angry, vengeful personality took over. She had emerged and believe me—she was no joke. When she was around, so was the evil presence that lurked in my dream. *It* was with me. I walked toward home as if I was floating on air. I was fearless.

There was a crowd at the end of the street of the school. I knew they were waiting on me. I smiled and pushed through until I was face to face with him. I gave him only seconds to step into the perimeter of my personal space. I pulled out both pencils and stabbed him as many times as I could. I don't remember any details after that. I'm not sure if he bled, I wasn't sure if he died, the only thing I remember is running toward home. Like any other time in my dream, I was being chased.

I later found out that he didn't die, but was injured. By the time the news reached me, I had already forgotten about the incident. My mom didn't say much, but I was forced to leave school and see a therapist. I thought victory was supposed to feel good.

It didn't.

My mom took me out of that school and placed me in a Christian one. She wanted me to start fresh. Not only was I a minority in race, but I was also secretly called a demon by some of the kids at this school because of my dark skin and I never seemed to fit in with anyone. If this was Jesus's school, my guess was if He ever did a surprise visit, the cigarette butts would disappear, name calling would stop, and the teachers would've cared more. The more I learned

Chapter Five – Dream Anxiety Disorder

about God, the less significant I felt, but my mom thought she was doing what was best. I couldn't bring myself to tell her about my cousins, or the new issues at the new school because I had already convinced myself that *I* was the common denominator.

Now, I was beginning to change. In my heart, I didn't want to hurt anyone; I didn't want to fight back. I just wanted it all to go away play my sports and enjoy my campfires. I came to the conclusion that everything was happening to me because I was the problem. The reason I was the problem is because I was evil. I tried to reason with myself, saying that I had a right to defend my body, just like my mom said, but that pleading went sour after I pulled out a pair of shears on my cousin Meech. He was fighting with his little brother over the Atari and he hit him a few times. It was clear to me that I did not like bullies. What was not clear to me is *why I was becoming something I didn't like.*

Spending the rest of the school year at the Christian school I was forced to attend taught me another lie. I learned from that school counselor, that God loves me differently and that is the reason I wasn't as pretty as everyone else. She said that God had a *special* plan for my life and that I shouldn't worry about what other kids were saying. Her attempt to console me included statements like; *I was not evil, I just looked different.* She pulled the Bible out and explained that *the reason evil demons attached themselves to me was because I was made for a greater purpose.*

Whatever, I thought. I didn't understand, nor did I care.

I decided that I didn't like that school, their beliefs, or the reason God made me. He'd clearly made a mistake and needed a do-over. The desire to die wasn't because I no longer wanted to live. I wanted to die because I didn't fully understand death. I no longer wanted people to do evil things to me and me to them, whether in my dream or my reality. To get rid of the problem was to get rid of the evil. To get rid of the evil was to get rid of its home.

Me.

I finally understood that I had to go.

So to die was a resolution of pain and a consideration for others. Never in a million years would I have taken the life of the only woman who loved me even more than I loved myself.

Nor did I really understand what death was.

Unfortunately, the internet wasn't around when I was that age, at least not that I know of. I remember playing Oregon Trails with the "new apple floppy disk" in computer class. My guess now is that if the World Wide Web did exist in my classroom at that time, I probably would've graciously tapped the infamous question in the Google box: "What is wrong with me?" All I knew for certain is that life was as it should be. I never projected any kind of hope outside of it.

Conclusion of Part One

So can you say Phew! I know that was a lot to take in for a first part. Thank you for reading and laughing, maybe even frowning. People have said to me that my story can be a little overwhelming. A lot of what I went through isn't verbalized that much in the general public.

I think it's crazy that it's not.

Especially with all of the secrets that are destroying our families and communities. As you can see in the first part of this book, I rarely mentioned names. When I did, they weren't real identities. When I first realized what I was purposed to do with my story and trainings, I was given very specific instructions from God. I know you're like, "Omg! He actually talked to you? Yes, but not in an audible voice, rather through His Word. But the instructions were very clear non-the-less. He said, in every story you tell, protect all reputations first.

I thought it would be rather important to invite you into the feelings and emotions of a child. I thought it would be note-worthy to share with you that suicide, bullying and abuse is two hundred times worse now than it was before. I was invited to speak at a youth summit at one of the local high schools. The school was in a suburban area and rated highly academically.

Part Two – The Transition

Chapter Six – Wait. She Did What?

People hear my story and if they know me personally, have a hard time connecting me with it. The person they see and know today is too happy and too positive to have come from such an experience. In their eyes, being able to overcome a tragedy of that magnitude is rare and close to impossible. It humbles me and I wear that badge of warrior proudly. What people don't know is that all I did was participate and desire to overcome. The real honor goes to God for healing, strengthening, and slowly guiding me through understanding, into remorse by acceptance and finally arriving at peace.

My past does not affect my behavior, personality, or heart flow. It used to. But now, I love hard, I love to help others, I'm positive, and I have crazy-sick faith that God created me the way He did, because He knew I was the one built for the assignment.

That being said, for those of you who are reading this book, I talk about my own relationship with God as it pertains to the 1611 King James Bible and according to that Bible. I am a Christian. I purposely made sure that this book was not labelled as such because it's too important to be labelled and placed with the other Christians-leading-other-Christians section. I want the people who don't believe to watch me. I want those who are straddling the fence and think that God doesn't want to have anything to do with them because of something they have done. The focus is not just on my faith. The focus is on how changing my expected future outcome, reflects my faith, leadership, servant hood and confidence by learning and developing who I am. Regardless of what I did or what I have been through, my past will never define me.

Justifiably, I shouldn't be here. You shouldn't be able to read positive affirming words from me because I was supposed to fail. People thought and said that I would fail by suicide, system, emotional turmoil, or institutionalized mentality. Why wouldn't they assume that? I had one case worker say to me that she didn't think that I would ever have children. She said that because my pain was so deep, I would never allow myself to love someone because I would never love myself enough and be able to forgive myself. Sadly, if I would've allowed that to become my reality, I wouldn't have the beautiful family that I do.

There has been some who knowingly entered my life and took advantage me. They thought I didn't know any better. I was hurt and disappointed by them and their behavior, but I didn't allow their behavior to change my objective. Did it alter the course of my relationship with them? Yes. But once I knew my life's objective, nothing could break or alter it. Not my past, not my relationships, and definitely not my current circumstances. Each and every experience is simply a negative or positive one. I decide to treat it as such and then move forward.

People have asked me, out loud, how could I overcome such a thing? How did I become so confident in who I am as a person after all I went through? My answer is all throughout this book. I am merely

Chapter Six – Wait. She Did What?

inviting you on a journey of healing, self-discovery, and perseverance.

While a memoir seemed more appropriate, it will have to wait because I'm afraid we don't have time. Too many of our youth are depressed. Too many single parents are defeated by the system and can't seem to get out of that seven year rut. Too many people are waking up defeated by life, pushing through the day with artificial stimulants and addicted to barcodes and knick knacks. You cannot become the leaders, parents, wives, husbands, and individuals you are supposed to be until a change is made at the very center of who you are. You need a confidence supercharge make over– so here I am.

I'm not superwoman for sure and I don't pretend to be, but I have come through some stuff that makes me responsible to share with others. I don't offer perfection, because just the other day, I would've loved to have sat my teenager's stuff outside and told her to figure it out because of the sarcasm in her tone. I'm still learning and I have allowed myself the idea that I will never stop learning. Becoming a student of life is the best change one can make.

Lastly, everything I offer is raw organic. I don't have case studies—though I do share examples from my own life. I don't have a degree in psychology—though I am a health/life coach. I don't have the average scholastic credentials to brag about. I have something better. I am made up of the confidence of a woman who can say to you that there are emotional and psychological laws that, to me, are merely a suggestion and that I have had to fall flat on my face to figure things out. I've had to wash, rinse and repeat bad relationships until I learned my worth. I've had to learn basic things the hard way that come very easily to most people. I offer pieces of me.

We have work to do. No matter who you are, where you come from, what you look like, who your mama or daddy is, or what you got, the very root of who you are will define what you become. If you lack confidence, you will fail. If you allow people to speak defeat into your life, you will fail. For a lot of us, we feel or have felt at one time that we would fail. We have to dig and lay some new foundation on purpose so that we can change that expected future outcome.

Murder, suicide, and death are all worst case scenarios. As one of those worst case scenarios, I am qualified to let you in on some secrets that most of you may be familiar with and some not-so-much. I get to brief you on the fact that aside from terrorism (the only exception to this rule), school shootings, suicides, juvenile murders, and parricides don't just happen one day.

They are "result based". Most of the time there is severe abuse, other times there is an unidentified mental disorder or both. I get to teach you the other side of the story because I fought my way through it.

I've had the opportunity, first hand, to sit in many groups with many girls with many issues more than once a day. I have been a part of and had an opportunity to lead those groups. I've had many therapists, social workers, mentors, and ministers, who were a part in helping me to piece all of it together. Now, I get to help shorten your learning curve.

There are two main characteristics which make my learning and teaching unique:

1. My initial foundation was uninterrupted. Being inside of an institution means no life interruption; bills, family, money and in-

dependence were things I really didn't have to worry about which left "self", "others", and how to relate with both.

2. I am a results expert. All of my tools and tactics are experienced based. They may not have been in book ready format at the time, but they were effective. Because of that effectiveness, I took the time to study theory and explanation over time. These methods have been worked by those who allowed me to walk or "coach" them through self-esteem enhancements.

This is not just "how-to" talk based on theories that I have read. There are four main areas where self-esteem killers are born or bred. These downers have preyed on us our entire lives. Every time we try to step out, up or make a better life for ourselves or our families, we are always interrupted. How you interact within these areas directly affect your esteem. They may be a part of your past, but they are also current issues. Strengthening confidence in these four areas will make a huge impact almost immediately, on bullying and abuse, parenting, relationships, and self.

What is important to remember is that **not having high self-esteem** is the same as **having low-self-esteem** especially in these areas. Self-awareness and confidence is an over-looked basic fundamental for managing life and its lemons. I endeavor to bring back its sexiness.

So pucker-up

Chapter Seven – YOU. Under Construction

Overcoming the Past and Rebuilding your Confidence *"From the Ground Up"* is only the beginning. This is an advanced crash course in self-confidence and re-direction. You may be one of the fortunate and not have a rough past to get over at all, but you do have a present life to keep smooth and in working order.

You will get to know me very well in this book. In fact, I may have to go into hiding for a while.

I'm kidding.

I only expose my stories to give you a different perspective, tug at your heart, or make you laugh. There is a lesson in everything that we encounter if we simply pay attention.

Consider this your own private cheerleading section. You have spent so much time, energy, and money making improvements to your atmosphere that you have forgotten about you. You matter. How you feel about yourself at the end of every day matters. How you feel will determine if it's worth another.

Embrace this journey because for once, it's all about you. When you reach the level of confidence that is needed to overcome the past, step into your purpose, and make whatever changes in your life that will make it your own, you will then have a desire to teach others to do the same. There is no greater feeling than to know that you truly make a difference in this life and that fact alone will affect many lives after this one.

Go ahead, grab your tool box, put on your hard hat, and say goodbye to anything that's been holding you back, for you are now officially "under construction".

Chapter Eight – Confidence is for Parenting

We sat in my almost-paid-off black Grand Am that housed graham crackers, water bottles, and old french fries. As a single parent, it was almost impossible to keep both my car and my apartment immaculate at the same time. When one sparkled and shined with cleanliness, the other consisted of strange and un-identified smells. Most of the time, the day would have me so beat, I couldn't do anything but sit.

I used to think that having better would make me feel better. I figured if I had a nice car, the fact that that it was nice would make me want to keep it clean; I felt like if it looked better, I would appreciate it. I came to realize that this is how most of us view our own self-worth. Confidence is destroyed based on what we feel we lack. This is far from true and it amazed me when I caught hold of it because we pass that down to our children. Then they grow up never feeling 'good enough'.

Imperfection is the best tool for learning. This lesson, along with a huge test of my own confidence, came strong and hard as I sat there in the car watching my fourteen-year-old daughter play with her new smartphone. I'm sure you'd agree, if you are a parent to a teen, that even those devices don't automatically initiate appreciation, until it's time for an upgrade.

We had just left a screening at Vineyard Columbus where we attended church. Church wasn't a new concept for me, but community was. The moment I stepped into the building, I felt a sense of community. Located next door is the community center where free classes and different community events take place. When, I saw the promotion for a mom and daughter screening, I immediately knew it was for me. The screening was a documentary film called "Yellow Roses". The film dealt with what our young girls face when it comes to bullying, abuse, and secrets. It was an amazing film in which teenagers themselves spoke out about how they were feeling and what they were going through in their lives, relationships and schools. They were also invited to discuss how they truly felt about the people in their lives–parents included–neglecting them during what seemed like the worst part of their lives.

The Vineyard Columbus made this screening available for anyone in the community who desired to learn more about what the challenges that our youth face are and why they do not typically disclose those challenges to parents or teachers. It was a platform that opened the door for discussion between teenage girls and their parents. If you are a parent, I highly recommend it. It is rare for a film to advocate problem solving and real issues in family life then offer suggestions on how to get started. It was genius.

I had been praying for a way to talk to my daughter about what I had been through and I always knew a way would be provided. My faith in God taught me all about witnessing and offering testimony but I knew that I couldn't come out to others with my story of struggle until I was able to tell my daughter what happened. That

Chapter Eight – Confidence is for Parenting

task alone was a test of my foundational confidence which is why I share it with you.

We sat in the car for a few moments playing on our smartphones. I knew this conversation needed to happen, I mentally prepared for what I was about to reveal. Based on the nature and impact of the film, I decided to take advantage of the platform offered. I powered down my device, turned and faced my daughter and said…

"So…what did you think about THAT for movie night?"…

As most teenagers would, she rolled her eyes knowing that avoiding or attempting to shorten the conversation would only make me talk more. She sighed, turned and faced me. She rolled her eyes and gave a gesture of the, "oh no, here-we-go attitude", so I was ready for the sarcasm.

Surprisingly, it never came.

"I thought it was interesting and a little crazy. What did you think?" she said sincerely.

That was a surprise. Either I misread her gesture or I assumed the worst. Either way I was relieved that she was open for discussion.

"It was a little crazy, but stuff like that really happens and young girls' lives are messed up and ruined forever because of those types of secrets. Sometimes young people don't feel like they have anyone to really go to and trust with information about what is going on in their world. They are afraid that they may be judged or in trouble for that information. Trying to navigate all of that drama, still keep grades decent, and be able to just laugh and have a good time seems like a lot of juggling for a kid, right?"

She hesitantly nodded her head. I took that as my cue to continue.

"I just want you to know that I love you and that I am safe for you to come to with any questions, concerns or sorting through this stage of your life. I won't judge you, punish you or be upset if you come to me with a situation that you are not sure how to handle. I would much rather you come to me versus anyone else because I will always tell you the truth no matter what. With other people that may not have good intentions or your best interest at heart, they could easily manipulate the truth to get you to do what they want. With me, you never have to worry about that because I am your mom and I want you to make mistakes, learn, and grow in the safety of my parenting, so that you can be and do the same for your daughter confidently—no matter how other parents seem to be doing it. I want to be your template for how moms should be so you can be that for your kids. I also want you to become the woman that God entrusted me to lead you to become". I stopped for a moment.

I could tell she was listening, even though she was playing with the buttons on her phone. I knew that this was the time to tell her and open that door that many of us parents are terrified to open: Confession. I learned long ago to choose my battles with her wisely and not often in order to gain her respect and trust. She wasn't a little girl anymore. I immediately went in for the kill,

"Are there any secrets that you want to share with me? Anything about school, someone you care for, or anything in general that you want to tell or ask me, but wasn't sure when or how, or afraid that if you did, I would be angry?" I asked.

"No", she said.

Chapter Eight – Confidence is for Parenting

My daughter and I are usually pretty open with each other. Even if I have to be the one to ask for the information because of discomfort, I know that once I ask, her answer will be straight up. I love that about her. What makes that even more awesome is that I am the one who planted that seed of *"how crucial it is to always tell the truth no matter how uncomfortable it may feel"* on the inside of her. In fact we kind of grew up together in a sense.

After I left the institution, I had her almost 9 months later. She became my world, my new focus and reason to succeed. I never let her leave my presence. I was always very protective of who held her and who interacted with her. I had definitely turned into my mom.

As she got older, so did her mentality. While I was trying to figure myself out in this new world, she was with me every step of the way. I allowed her to have an input on major decisions because it was just the two of us. Although I had a wonderful church family, it took a long time for me to allow anyone close to either of us. Therefore, my daughter became my best friend. I had natural and learned motherly instincts that helped in creating the boundaries that were necessary. I also studied and read a lot about parenting while I was pregnant because everything outside of the institution was new for me. I dove into every learning experience as if I was in a whole new world because it was.

I protected my daughter with my life. I watched her moods and learned her habits. In return, she saw my strengths and my weaknesses, she watched my drive and determination and she picked up on my lack of trust towards other people. She saw me through all of my career changes, confidence building, my marriage, divorce, and the birth of my middle son.

We ended up in a homeless shelter a few years prior because I walked away from a job in a different state for standing up for what I believe, she was a witness to this and used my own words of strength and perseverance to encourage and remind me of who I was and what I stood for. She reminded me that I had been through hard times before and that this was just another test I had to pass to go to the next level. Her young brain and old wisdom pieced together what it takes most people years to figure out;

"Everything in life has a time for its function and a cycle is a round motion, not a flat line and therefore it cannot continue to remain the same forever."

My fourteen-year-old understood seasons.

What that showed me is not only did she actually listen to me sometimes, but she watched every decision, every mistake and every victory that affect our lives, how I adapted and brought us out of them. She willed me back into what I thought I lost when I hit rock bottom and caused us to be homeless. She knew that I hadn't lost my will to move forward, but that it just wasn't clear in the midst of the mess.

My fourteen-year-old understood endurance.

I always knew that we had a special relationship and that we could talk about anything, so it did not surprise me that she didn't have any secrets. The few instances and situations in her life that could've been a secret, she came to me and talked with me about them immediately. She was definitely uncomfortable, but "worded" her way through it. I was very intent on not ruining the opportunity because if I would have, it would be a long time before I'd be offered another one.

Chapter Eight – Confidence is for Parenting

This particular night was about my secret and I knew that it was time to share it with her. My secrets had a purpose to fulfill, and if I did what I was supposed to as a parent to her, she would be on board and ready. This was the test.

"Well, I have a secret that I need to tell you", I said.

She became uninterested in the buttons on her phone and I had her direct and full attention. Up until this time, I hadn't disclosed everything that I went through in my childhood. I, instead, used my experiences carefully and as it related to the situation at the time that it did. For instance, there were girls at her previous school who cut on their arm. When she told me about it, I knew it was time to share with her that I used to do the same, what could be going on in the lives of kids who do that and what the kids may feel when they do it.

She never really seemed shocked or disappointed when I shared bits and pieces of my past but as time went on her wisdom grew along with her intellect through the sharing of information about my life. Telling her about difficult moments in my own past gave her a different perspective than a lot of her peers. This activated empathy, concern and a reaching out mentality as opposed to a bully or unconcerned student. She never looked down on someone else because of what they looked like or if what they were doing was considered "weird" or abnormal. This mindset has become a part of her character, and for that I am proud.

My fourteen-year-old understood compassion.

I knew that it was time to take all of those little experiences that I had previously shared with her and drive them home to the big picture. For the first time in a very long time, I verbally expressed what went on that last year before the incident.

And I did.

Sitting in the car, I told her everything. I started off by saying, *"remember when I told you that I was sexually abused as a child?"* and went on through my life in chronological order leading up to my attempted suicide and the accident with my mom. I'm not really sure what I expected from her or that I even had an expectation. I just knew that a lot of what I went through at that age seems to now be considered a "norm."

The things that are happening now in the lives of our teenagers are ten times worse, more advanced, and have fatal consequences. I wanted to convey to her that having a desire to end my life as a child was not normal and how the statistics are alarming now and kids are actually dying by their own choice. I explained to her that taking my mother's life was not intended, understood, or on purpose. I went on to say that I was a little younger than her and could not articulate what I was feeling. I told her by not having someone in my corner who knew me well enough to dig and piece together the elements of my distress or fight for my freedom, I had to face the consequences and be placed in the institution for the rest of my childhood life.

I made very clear that secrets held by children are unsafe. I referenced a few examples in the film we had seen moments before and referred back to a time where I told her that she couldn't close her bedroom door while she had company. I shared my belief that kids shouldn't be introduced to "privacy" because they can't mentally handle the responsibility of it. I told her what went on behind

Chapter Eight – Confidence is for Parenting

closed doors that hurt and affected me as a child when I was told to keep it a secret. I didn't leave anything out or try to screen my words because the words I chose not to screen are the ones that have become common conversation for her peer group.

I held back as many tears as I could. The few that fell weren't because I was sad; they were empathy tears. I knew that it was time to share my story with others so that they could have hope for themselves. Those tears represented a powerful understanding of strength and I wanted them to spill over into a container, sealed with all the answers that she would need for her life. I wanted them to be preventative so that she would never have to encounter the situations that I revealed and the teenagers from the film had to face. They were also tears of honor because I felt 'chosen' for my bounce-back. I couldn't find the words to make her understand that with this rebound, came responsibility. I told her that I wanted her to know everything before I stepped onto any platform and shared my life. I first had to include the most important person of all.

Her.

When I stopped talking, she looked up at me with tears in her eyes. She too, wasn't crying because she was sad; she admitted to being upset that I had to go through all of that, but she was mostly proud that I made it through. We held each other for a little while and I asked her what has brought me to this very moment with you as my reader.

"With everything I have been through, I believe that God has been training me directly and indirectly so that I can help others. I really didn't have a training ground to rebuild my self-confidence to where I could feel like I at least had the same opportunities as anyone else, so

everything I learned was self-taught. I believe that the reason I couldn't find contentment in all of the awesome career fields I have been in is because what I am really supposed to be doing will cause a bigger impact. Those opportunities were for me to help train others."

I continued. *"I would never want anyone to live with the feeling of low self-worth and defeated confidence that I did for so long. This means that people need to hear my story; they will know what I have been though, what I did, and it will give them hope that they too can overcome. I am just wondering if you are okay with that."*

She too was in tears. She nodded, and said *"Yes, you have to. If you don't, they won't know what to do".*

This was an important moment for me. I wasn't asking for my teenager's approval to fulfill my purpose and begin on my path. I was asking for the support of my daughter so that she too can learn and develop into the woman that I know she will become because of how I decided to NOT give up on life.

Opening the lines of communication is so relevant and powerful because our children have to learn to communicate at an early age without the fear of saying the wrong thing or saying it in the wrong way.

Freedom of expression is what I taught my daughter. Does it have to be tamed sometimes? Yes.

But are there content boundaries? No. Never.

Because even the worst situation in a teenagers life deserves the attention and brainstorming with a trusted parent or guardian who may not always agree, but promises to let love lead the conversation and wisdom to have input.

Chapter Eight – Confidence is for Parenting

My fourteen-year-old understood effective communication.

She now also understands *me*.

Chapter Nine – The Silent War Against Parents

The world is changing. Our kids live in a totally different culture than what we grew up in. They are not only required, but expected, to learn more things faster and through more channels and outlets. When we send them to school we have to trust that what we teach them in our presence is implemented when they are not. We cannot depend on our school systems and church organizations to teach all and be all to our children, that's our job as parents. We are their first line of command. Our children have been watching our every move since their eyes could focus. The saying goes "they may not always do what we say, but they always do what we do".

As that first line of command, you sometimes feel defeated. It appears as if our children's friends, coaches, and everyone else's opinion and advice matters to them but yours. This is a normal resistance, especially as a parent to a teenager. I know firsthand what it is like to take the time to try and explain something to her that will save her years of destruction only for her to roll her eyes and act as if she isn't listening. To add insult to injury, someone *else* will tell her the exact same thing I did and she listens with intent and interest. She then regurgitates the information back to me as if our conversation never happened at all. After talking with many other parents with teens, I know for a fact we are not alone in this war on communication and I can assure you that they are listening, even when we think they are not.

Confidence as a parent is mandatory. We are replicating ourselves and creating generations. In marriage where parenting plays a part, it is important to work as a team with your spouse– accepting and honoring each other's role in the marriage. Our children learn how to be husbands and wives based on how you show them it should look. Our kids watch how we handle conflict, disagreement, and home management and they will take on that role in their own lives and marriages.

Scenario One: *There is a heated discussion between mom and dad. During that disagreement, mom is fiercely yelling and cursing at dad, challenging his decisions and refusing his leadership. Dad retracts to the bedroom. Both son and daughter are present when this heated discussion spirals out of control. They appear to be a little upset, but most likely nothing traumatic. They may not have appeared to be affected directly when this happens because disagreements, we teach them, are a part of life and that sometimes moms and dads fight.*

What you later witness is that the daughter takes on a very strong, dominant personality and tries to control her relationships. She doesn't respect men and yells and curses as a way to resolve conflict. She is not capable of operating in a healthy, long-term relationship which will ultimately lead to her disappointment and heartbreak.

In the son's relationships there appears to be peace, but its surface. He has mastered submissive behavior. He doesn't challenge *any* woman in a relationship in an effort to avoid conflict altogether.

Chapter Nine – The Silent War Against Parents

He learned that running and hiding from a problem in a relationship is how to avoid arguments. He will never be a leader is his home.

Both will lead to an identity crisis on a search to find the answers to the questions about themselves that they could only receive from their parents.

Challenges we face as a parents have a direct effect on our confidence levels. We are not perfect, yet we try to be. Except we don't know any other perfect parent, so where is our standard?

Self-esteem is also tampered with if you allow your kids to talk back, disobey and challenge your instruction that eventually leads to lack of balance and authority. The lack of authority turns into disrespect and ultimately effects how you see yourself as a parent, then not long after that, an individual.

We go on this tangent thinking that we are in complete control of our kids. A lot of times it's because of fear and not wanting them to make similar mistakes to the ones we made. Other times, we lack control in virtually every other area of our lives and feel like we have a sense of ownership to our kids because we birthed them. When our teenagers were young children, creating boundaries came naturally and most of the time without explanation or instruction. Even at a young age, they understood that we *are* the boundary and what we say was how it would go. No questions. As toddlers, they begin to form an opinion. Now, not only do they have an answer for everything, but they also talk back. Some parents become submissive to their own children, when really-the toddler stage is the time to stand our ground and not give in to their cute little faces (I still struggle in that department).

Adolescence changes the game completely. As parents to teenagers, we are constantly trying to create boundaries and at the same time adjust them because they need to build trust and learn on their own. We want to scream and fight with them to assert our authority. We do that because we love them and really want to prevent them from hitting the brick wall that we see, that they don't. It was foreign to me when a friend of mine told me that I needed to choose my battles with my daughter because for me every time she disobeyed or mouthed off—the battle began. It never occurred to me that I needed to actually 'hear' or 'care about' her opinion. I always considered myself as a student in this world and if I struggled in an area and someone offered a solution, I tried it. When I did, it made such a huge difference in our relationship. There are still times that she may really want to do something that I don't believe is a good idea. I know for a fact it will cause some future hardship either in her spirit or in her environment. When she gives the opposing argument, her stand is also strong—from a teen point of view. So I have had to help build her confidence by allowing her point-of-view to have victory. When it turned out not to be a victory—but instead a hardship, I have to refrain from the "I-told-you-so-speech", stand alongside of her pick up the pieces. The return on that exchange is priceless.

I am aware that there is a silent war on parenting. Parents are being stripped of their authority and being told to not discipline their child. They are being told not to spank their children, get in their faces, or discipline them when they are wrong or disrespectful. The imbalance against that logic is if our children are not reverentially fearful of us, like we should be of God—then why would they respect anyone else? Unfortunately time-outs are not universally effective, especially with a strong-willed child. As long as parents feel that they are not permitted to parent, the war will continue. Is there a line between discipline and abuse? Of course. But a good parent is obvious by the character of their child not the circumstance of the discipline.

There are two types of abusive parents that carry a parenting style of extremely aggressive or extremely passive. Extremely aggressive is most obvious and includes a lot of cursing, screaming, and most of the time physical harm. An extremely passive parent is more along the lines of a manipulator. A manipulative parent uses a child to get them to do whatever will benefit that parent. These parents seem not to care what their children do unless it affects them directly. These parents feel like they want to give their child space and not be in their business. They have an extreme false trust of their child and expect the child to respect and honor them because they don't "interfere" or "get in their business".

This logic is lacks parental balance.

By not being in your child's *business* or interfering in their life, not only are you telling them subliminally that you don't love them, but they become a higher risk for everything you fear for them as a parent. This type of freedom is false because it only involves surface level communication which can easily be manipulated and a foundation for the "secrets" that they have to keep. We are sometimes more willing to accept a *verbal*: "no, I'm not having sex yet" rather than question the obvious red flags (i.e., condoms in pockets and emotional outbursts). Those children lead lives of confusion and discontent. They have no sense of identity or character. They go through life always trying to figure out who they are and what they are here for. When children are trying to find the answers to life's questions, we not only need to become the expert but the researcher and validator as well. If you sense that you may be an abusive parent, or were at one point, all is not lost.

We do the best with what we know and have, from this point; it's all about forward movement.

Chapter Ten – Taking Back Our Parental Authority

I commend those parents who go through backpacks, listen in on conversations, and know the name and parents of their child's friends. You are doing what you are supposed to. Thank you to those parents who demand obedience and enforce discipline. You may not be their favorite person now, but behind bars "favorite" is irrelevant. And to those parents, who do have to communicate through a glass window, let go of the guilt and condemnation because you did the best with what you understood. Every child becomes an adult and understanding right and wrong is taught enough outside the home for them to know the difference.

For the parents who teach and display personal boundaries—you are appreciated because your daughters are less likely to engage in the physical or emotional abuse of a boyfriend. If they just so happen to stumble upon one with some of those characteristics, alarms will sound and she will make the decision to walk away with no hesitation. Those daughters become well-rounded women who know that a better man is out there, even if it means waiting longer than they originally desired.

Your sons may not like the idea of boundaries but they will recognize when theirs are being crossed. They won't allow their girlfriends to control the relationship. He will appreciate the uniqueness of his wife and lead her and his family without losing the strength of his manhood. Years later, they will return to the nest with honor, wisdom, and deep gratitude.

No one is perfect.

Parents are not perfect and children will not be either.

You only need to understand your role and how having a healthy sense of self-esteem makes you the best parent you can be. Strive for that level of parenting. Once your children realize how imperfect you are, but how you love them and give them worth—they will then relate to that imperfection when they become parents and pass the fundamentals downward. This is building and leading a generation.

Rebuilding your individual confidence puts you on the path of becoming a confident parent, even if your parents were not. Throughout this book, you will adapt to what's current and acquire the tools you need to manage your home the way it will work for you and your family.

Parents like you and I believe, in spite of our past abuse or present mistakes that we have a voice. That voice is the leading of wisdom in our own parenting. How do we find it? What does it look like? Parents who deliberately make a decision to take back their authority:

- Communicate with their children about abuse and bullying and create a game plan.

Chapter Ten – Taking Back Our Parental Authority

- Call out the secrets that destroy self-esteem and confidence in their sons and daughters.
- Drill into their teenage daughters that beauty and strength is not defined by how much you weigh or what your body type is, but who you are when no one is looking and how you treat others.
- Teach their children that character, hard work and the ability to learn and focus will shape them into who they are supposed to be.
- Teach their sons that men are judged by their character and how well they provide for their children with or without the other parent's involvement.
- Make themselves heard in leading by example.
- Put away the molesters in the family.
- Pull together as a community and not only train their children, but other children if needed, to fight back.

I am not only a survivor of bullying and abuse; I am also a mother of a teenage girl. I didn't realize how much I really didn't understand as a twelve-year-old until I walked with my daughter through that year. I see a lot of the same attacks that are forming against our youth and it has caused an outrage in my spirit.

This generation of youth can and will fight back. They will step out and try new things regardless of danger and warning signs. They are forming anti-bulling campaigns around the world and are coming together to take a stand. They are tweeting, making comments, snapping photos, and showcasing their feelings on You Tube. They have the desire to make changes, they just need direction. As a parent, you must be confident in order to lead and show them the way

Chapter Eleven – Why Parents Need Trained in Confidence

You are brave beyond measure for taking part in this movement. You want to feel good about who you are, what you have been through and what you stand for. You have a strong desire to step up and take on the responsibility of leadership as a parent and you want to be an excellent one where the return is not monetary, but in how well your children do the same with their children.

This is your answer to the beginning of a new foundation. Alterations, change, and improvement never have expiration dates. That's why there will always, always, always be a newer version of a cell phone and a newer, upgraded version of a computer. You have wandered long enough in distraction. Put down the business plan, cut hours on the job, and be present with your children. No more excuses. We only have them for 18 years and that time flies by extremely fast.

Now that we understand and relate to what it takes to be confident, it's time to get about the business of doing it and making it happen. This is only the beginning. This journey is important from this day forward because you will be open and subject to criticism like never before. Un- confident parents, parents who pretend to have confidence, or the bullying parents of our children's peers, manipulators, and abusers are extremely uncomfortable around confident people. They feel threated and intimidated by a confident person's strength, opinion, and aura. I'm here to tell you that that is okay.

The word foundation is where we will start. As children, we may not have had the control or brain function to understand what it was we needed to grow into productive and positive leaders. Somehow along the way whatever it was that we lacked, we figured out how to get it. Psychologists refer to this as a high *self-efficacy*.

Wikipedia defines self-efficacy as: *The measure of the belief in one's own ability to complete tasks and reach goals.*

It goes on to say that:

Self-efficacy affects every area of human endeavor. By determining the beliefs a person holds regarding his or her power to affect situations, it strongly influences both the power a person actually has to face challenges competently and the choices a person is most likely to make.

If you are reading this book and you want to embrace the journey ahead, you have a seed of self-efficacy. You are strong, rare, and are a leader in the making that strives for excellence and moral best practices. You understand that parenting is a gift. One that could expire or snatched away very quickly.

As a parental leader in what I call the "Fight Back" industry (which I will explain later on in this book), you will emerge, learn, grow, and find yourself within yourself. When you do, you will be more

Chapter Eleven – Why Parents Need Trained in Confidence

fulfilled, have a sense of purpose and your life will change, as will how you see your children and your parenting.

You would think that as a mom to a fourteen-year-old, I would have mastered this, but I have not. Mostly because parenting is "on-the-job-training", it's my first time with a teenager and I know my results won't be for years down the line. You know after the crazy hormones. On a surface level, confidence has a feelings-based confirmation. Until the proper work is done, your progress within yourself will only be guided by how you "feel" about yourself.

As you gain deeper meaning and apply more learning tools, your confidence levels will shift from feelings-based to identity-based. This is where I will lead you to. Identity based confidence will cause you to have new ideas and possibilities that you never thought you would.

I have mastered self-confidence mostly due to lack of distraction and I believe there is gifting involved so that I can teach others. While I was in the juvenile facility, I had the opportunity to learn, implement, teach, and repeat that process with hundreds of girls. I received feedback, discipline, and different tools daily without the normal interruption of life. I didn't have to worry about bills, food, and clothing. All I had to do was focus on my personal growth, education and development. I did that twenty-four hours a day, seven days a week for eight years.

When I was released at age twenty-one, I had to utilize those tools that I had become accustomed to. Because it was real life and my environment was not controlled, I had to quickly adapt to and create other weapons and tools. Because I understood the concept and had established the foundation of creating tools for myself, adapting and creating was second nature.

I have accepted who I am and what I stand for as a parent. I understand my beliefs and why I believe the way I do and I am confident enough to teach those beliefs to my children and will not lose confidence if they choose to later believe differently. Not because I have a large ego and my way is right—because I don't, and it's not. I have learned that no one way of anything is the right way because we all come from different mentalities, environments, structures, and systems. We all have a different view of what this should look like. Lacking confidence requires us to crave a "standard" something or someone to measure ourselves by or be measured against. This leads to extreme emotional disappointment.

Let's visit the highly esteemed parents of Lucrative Estates Middle School (yes, I totally made that up), a place where designer clothes are expected and birthday invitations are based on whether or not the community you live in is gated. Your child earns a full scholarship to that school because of their talent and recommendation from an athletic scout that saw them at a school game. This is a fabulous opportunity, everyone is excited. Unfortunately, students with scholarships who attend the school are cast out and shunned because a scholarship is seen as a hand out.

As a parent, though, you are proud and couldn't be happier. The school PTA is looking for parents to help out and the recruiter that chose your child throws a party. You are ecstatic because your child receiving that scholarship allowed you more time to be involved. You no longer have to pick up more hours at work or find a second job. You can now spend that time being involved. The party is wonderfully set up, there is plenty of food and parents from the school seem to be enjoying themselves.

Everyone but you.

Chapter Eleven – Why Parents Need Trained in Confidence

All the other parents appear to be dressed and put together like supermodels. You did the best with what you had. Normally, you like the way you dress. Normally, you are a free-spirited person and have the boldness to mingle and the gift of gab.

Not tonight.

Tonight—they stole your "normally".

Allowing me to lead you in this journey will bring out the parent you want to be. It will give you the tools you require to hold on to your way of parenting so that other people's ideas and concepts can be filtered appropriately and you can alter and receive ideas and concepts without feeling inadequate or like you have to dig and re-build your foundation.

Because we are a community and a lot of parents are not exposed to other communities and ways of doing things, I have collected a snapshot of what a confident parent looks like. This snapshot has come from years of watching, implementing, failing, succeeding, and following other classes of parents–that if not done purposely, I would have never been exposed to new ideas or alternative ways of seeing things. I had to do the groundwork because I was at a very young age when my environment became controlled, so the only idea of parenting I had was that of my own family. Though, there was some good, most of it was not and that was my first lesson in filtering. As of now, I take on the role of this snapshot as a parent and this was my original foundation.

When I give you this snapshot of what a confident parent looks like, feel free to build from my list and tweak what I may lack due to your own personal experiences. Once you learn the five tools in depth, you will be able to apply their function while having a picture of what you are trying to create. This is what *From the Ground Up* is all about. Overseeing your progress as you build your custom foundation while offering you tools to defend your vision. From this moment on, you are a parent who is like no other. Your children will grow and evolve because you have taken back the authority that you thought they were ready for, you are no longer passive or aggressive and from this moment on, you are not to be taken lightly.

The Snapshot of a Confident Parent:

1. A confident parent loves first and foremost. They demonstrate positive affection verbally, physically, and on purpose. They display love in both action and words regardless of how they feel at the time. They love unconditionally regardless of performance, abilities, or inabilities, and display of behavior in their children.

In my experiences all children perceive and receive love differently. Because I have three, it was important to take the time to understand each one's perception on love and use that as my demonstration of it.

This concept came from one of my favorite books called *The Five Love Languages* by Gary Chapman. His concept as received by me was that because we come with different souls and personalities we receive love in different forms. The five love languages that he presents are quality time, words of affirmation, physical touch, receiving of gifts, and acts of service.

These languages are selfless and very unique to the individual to whom they belong. You can have more than one, but there is still a primary love language that makes you feel loved the most.

Chapter Eleven – Why Parents Need Trained in Confidence

According to *The Five Love Languages*, my daughter's love language is receiving of gifts. What that means is, no matter how much I verbally express love to her by telling her I love her and how beautiful she is (words of affirmation) she will feel loved the most by me if I put it in a card or write it on stationary and place it in an unopened source on her bed. Receiving something from me is how she feels loved the most.

My son, on the other hand, always asks me to buy him stuff. Of course, not even three hours later, I find that thing I bought in the middle of the floor where sometimes I am lucky enough to dodge it and sometimes not-so-much. It didn't take long to figure out that, no matter what he is involved with or doing, as soon as I sit down he is right up under me, laying on me or hugging on me—his love language is physical touch. So this means that no matter how much I show up at the school in his classroom as a room parent volunteer watching him from the sidelines while still being in his presence (quality time), allowing him to hold my hand or sit on my lap will make him feel most loved.

For children, love is their first foundation even before confidence because if they don't know what love should feel and be like, they will not be introduced to self-love and therefore will not learn how to turn it into confidence.

I recommend this book to every parent who has a desire and an interest in digging deep into the heart of their children. There is a *Five Love Languages for Children, Couples* and, more recently, a *Military* edition.

  1. A confident parent creates order and teaches boundaries on a daily bases. They understand that organization is part of

parenting and is necessary for training and developing a child who will one day be an adult and must learn order and how to prioritize. They teach boundaries so that their children learn what is and is not okay when it comes to their personal space and life. This also begins the lesson on responsibility for their environment (cleaning up after one's self), adjusting to seasons (wearing shorts in 2 feet of snow not a good idea) and communicating limitations involving other people (telling someone that it is not okay to touch them inappropriately vs. telling the doctor no during a necessary exam). Without this foundation, chaos and confusion forms in a child's environment, verbal and physical expression, and feelings and they never learn that it is not ok to always say what they feel at the time they want to say it. They also lack the ability to say "no" when saying "no" is needed. Lastly, it is this foundation that prepares them for healthy balanced relationships with other people.

I use to struggle with this one a lot. In the 2005 version of the American Family film "Yours, Mine and Ours" I used to be a replica of Rene Russo's character, Helen, when it came to her style of parenting. She believed in freedom of expression and communication with very little or no strict order or discipline.

In one of the scenes she says something along the lines of *"home is to be a place where the kids can openly express themselves without fear of being judged or reprimanded."* Her six kids in the movie are adopted and come from all different cultures and backgrounds, their personalities are distinct, recognizable, and individually appreciated. Their freedom of expression includes spray painting the walls, fixing their own breakfast, and being comfortable with the extracurricular activities they are into.

Chapter Eleven – Why Parents Need Trained in Confidence

Her co-star and ex-widowed husband Frank, played by Dennis Quaid, was the extreme opposite. He had a military background and his six kids were disciplined, communicative, neat and orderly. They were high school sweethearts who both wanted big families but lost touch. During their reunion they fell in love again, got married that night, told the kids the next day and moved everyone in together. As you can imagine it was a mess and put a lot of pressure on them as a large family.

Freedom of expression is part of my personality style, but organization and not acting on impulse came very hard for me. When I was married, my ex-husband and I drove each other crazy. Not because we didn't appreciate each other's personality or love each other but he and I resembled that union in the movie. We didn't know how to live together in a home and we both lacked the confidence level that is needed in a marriage to work together to come up with a solution even if it means three or four failed attempts.

After I recognized that there had to be a larger source or root to my impulses than an expressive nature and adventurous personality, I began to search for answers. Researching and reaching out for answers came easy to me because I was trained to do so. But living in an environment where other factors such as divorce, heartbreak, and childbirth are thrown into the equation, it becomes very hard to focus on me and my needs. I later learned that that lack of focus was not just me, but Adult ADHD.

Making reference to the movie and disclosing a diagnosis does not mean that as parents that we have to be one way or the other in order to be good parents. Nor do we need to attempt to self-diagnose because someone else tells us that something is wrong with our social style. The point that I am making here is that part of what I am teaching you will help you to understand who you are as an individual which will help you to understand how you think and why, so that you can accept that person in the mirror, make only the adjustments you desire, and then teach your kids to do the same.

When I became a *single* parent, I had to learn organizational skills on purpose, and seek help to conquer the other stuff. If done correctly, research, outside help, and support will enhance-not destroy-your confidence.

Setting boundaries and teaching our children how to do the same is the best practice we can teach them. Not only will this foundation come in handy as an adult, but teaching them this skill, keeps them out of possible harm and danger as well. The one thing that a cyber-bully and their victim have in common is a lack of boundaries. Yes, as parents it is our responsibility to not only know and store passwords to all things social and online, but to also know when to give our kids a break from technology period. Most of the time a cyber-bully is effective because they have 24-hour access to their victim.

1. A confident parent enforces rules and disciplines in the way that is most appropriate for each individual child without influence from anyone outside of the home. This parent creates that discipline for the individual child and with the greater good of the household in mind. They agree that saying no is not only ok, but expected. They explain why rules are formed, how rules become laws and the consequences of ignoring, manipulating and not following them. They can ignore pouting and tantrums when they need to and address them when it is

necessary. They are also capable of knowing when it is and is not ok to follow through on discipline thus showing and teaching empathy and mercy.

I used to receive a lot of criticism when I spoke on spanking as a form of discipline for my son. But by that time I already had a confident foundation and could withstand the opinion and thoughts of other people. Because of my "destroying the box" mentality (which you will learn later) I was able to gain a 360 degree perception on discipline, his personality, and the dangers of lack of discipline and best and worst case scenarios all at the same time.

I know there will be some of you who will disagree with me and some of you will be on board one hundred percent. Either way, your opinion is irrelevant to my discipline style. Not because I don't care, but because my foundation is different from yours as yours will be from everyone else's and when it comes to a family unit, the ways and practices of that family should never be rocked or destroyed because of an opinion of an outsider.

That being said, I will explain to you for learning purposes my stand. I was abused as a child by other members in my family. However, I was disciplined in my home by my mom. Even at a young age, the spankings I received were necessary, effective, and the punishment usually fit the crime. I didn't get spanked often and never out of anger. I did not become violent because of those spankings and therefore was not abused.

I have sat in groups where eleven to sixteen year olds talked about being beaten by objects, manipulated with food, and crushed by words. I've heard thousands of these stories about these and worse things being done to kids in their own words. Those kids turned into juvenile offenders and committed crimes that hurt other people, including murder, because that type of damaging violence had been done to them

I know firsthand what abuse is and what it's not. My son displayed a very demanding and strong willed nature as a two year old. I understood his soul as a little boy and I allowed room for adventure, destruction, and warzones. He never got in trouble for climbing on the counter to get something out that he wasn't really supposed to have. We just shook our head when he broke something in the house and learned to put away what we didn't want destroyed. We took his not wanting to eat his veggies as a sign of stubbornness because we introduced vegetables to him as a baby so they were not foreign. He had just developed an opinion about what he wanted and did not want to eat, so sometimes we made him sit there until he ate, or we took away a desert or snack. But we never made an *alternate* meal.

Around age four, after we made it very clear that he is to immediately stop what he is doing and come when we call him, he naturally tested boundaries. Sometimes, he would ignore us and continue to do whatever it was he was doing until he got ready to come. Other times he came after the third or fourth time we would call out to him and after trying other ways of discipline, we decided that because the behavior was not only disobedience, but a test of our authority and what we considered to be unsafe.

I gave him some swats on his bottom which hurt his feelings and pride more than his behind and he cried until he fell asleep. We had two more instances after that between ages five and eight and never again since. The swatting on the butt worked for us and for him in

Chapter Eleven – Why Parents Need Trained in Confidence

that situation and it corrected a behavior that was taking too long to correct and in our opinion became a safety issue.

Each time he was reprimanded we explained to him why and the importance of coming when we call him. I would always give the example of the bad person that breaks into the house to steal something or hurt us that he remembers to this day. I explained to him that if I put him in a hiding place and tell him not to move, make any noises, or come out until someone safe finds him, his obedience could mean life or death. Thank God that was a drill we never had to practice, but our way of dealing with his disobedience worked for us and him. Other than normal little boy stuff, at age nine, we no longer have an issue with disobedience.

Although adjustments are necessary and are a part of learning how to be a parent, it is crucial for a parent to remain as consistent as possible in order to build a solid foundation in their children. All over the place parents breed all over the place children and all over the place children become jacks of all trades and masters of none.

I share my method as an example because my results speak for themselves. I have a very well-behaved and respectful nine-year-old. Having confidence as a parent means believing in your ability to know what's best for your children and be able to defend that no matter what.

1. A confident parent learns to master the art of all forms of communication. Yes, even the newer ones like texting and twitter. These parents are most definitely in their kids business all the time. They understand that in American culture, even at the age of thirteen, a child is not ready to put on a backpack,

travel alone to and wander on the streets of New York City —no matter how adventurous it sounds. They compare the same concept to the navigation of the World Wide Web and treat it the same way.

These parents watch and listen from a distance and when the time is right, sensed or summonsed, offer their input on any given topic involving the social life of their children. These parents communicate rules, expectations and only offer explanation when a lesson is to be learned and does not offer one if one isn't needed.

It's true. There is a time where because "I said so" is appropriate. Not because we don't want our child to understand why we set the rules we set and do the things we do, but because they won't always understand, and they shouldn't have to try and figure it out all of the time either. Other times our communication is vital in their training because they are at a point to where they can understand and reason with the rules we set and even as they get older challenging those rules should be safe and encouraged when appropriate.

Because children who have been bullied, are witness to it, or are the bully themselves tend to hide that situation very well when at home away from their school environment, communication is the only way to learn about how much your child does know about it firsthand. Most parents find themselves in a situation where they are both appalled and baffled to find out that their child is either a victim of bullying or abuse or is the bully or abuser.

There will not always be obvious signs and some of the time the signs will be so obvious that fear stops the parent from digging deeper. Talking with them about everything with no restrictions opens the

Chapter Eleven – Why Parents Need Trained in Confidence

line of communication and therefore offers a platform for admission. We almost all of the time have to be the initiators. What's even more important is how we react. In mastering communication as a parent, we are able to control our verbal and non-verbal communication when we receive disturbing information from our children. This is crucial because it will set the tone of them coming to us with more things to talk about. This is a practice that will take time and effort, especially as a mother.

Hard to practice? Yes.

Possible to master? Absolutely.

Results? Priceless.

1. A confident parent takes the time to learn, understand and listen to their children. They easily adapt to their child's maturity offering respect and understanding. They know when to step into a situation and when to allow training time for their child. At the same time, they also know when to stand up for and defend their child regardless of consequence or fear. They understand that in order for a child to mimic a behavior, they have to first witness it in action.

My daughter was really into Anime, a Japanese cartoon concept. As a Christian parent, I immediately came against it because of the cultural difference behind the making of it and at thirteen didn't really offer her too much explanation. That was just the rule and the rule was set. The following year, she came to me and asked me what I did not like about it and we had a discussion where I talked, she listened, and vice versa. We came to a common ground of the types of Anime that would be appropriate enough for her to handle and I let up off of it. First of all, after I banned it from the house, I never gave it a second thought, but apparently this new emerging hobby became important enough for her to check back in with me. I instilled that thought process in her. I always told her that we are communicators, and even if there is something very uncomfortable that she needs to talk about, I am open and willing to have that discussion -no filters.

This comes in handy with sex, drugs, smoking, and anything else that teenagers are into these days. If they can't come to us with the questions and concerns so that they can at least have the understanding of the situations so they can make a decision, who else will they go to? And how dare we get bothered by a decision they made when the consequences both good and bad were never made clear. It is our responsibility to make sure our children can identify and name their body parts, understand the positive and negative consequences of drug use and abuse, sex, drinking, and disobedience of authority, expose them to our past so they can understand that most of the time we speak from experience and not do not always get our ideas from Dr. Phil or The Lifetime Channel. We also need to teach and set the example of what healthy and unhealthy relationships look like so they will be able to recognize and judge them for themselves.

Parental confidence gives you the ability to teach your children how to live this life and navigate its troubles and layers, then trust our children with that information allowing them to grow and form their own values and belief systems for their families. A confident parent is not controlling and does not have the desire to make their child's life miserable and call it teaching them a lesson.

Chapter Eleven – Why Parents Need Trained in Confidence

You are on the way to being a confident parent. I know that you already have what it takes because you are still reading this book even though your opinion may differ from mine and you may implement some things differently or add more of your own—you are a parent who is committed to a level of excellence that not every parent will be committed to.

Parenting a teenager doesn't have to be as complicated as we make it. There are plenty of times that I made mistakes, screwed up, and had to redeem myself. I was one of those parents who demanded that the kids went and played in their room and then yelled at them to pick the toys up off of the floor ten minutes later.

I encourage you to go slow and take the time to understand the concept of confidence before trying to teach it to your children. Why? Let use a simple yet relevant example of an emergency on an aircraft. In order for you to assist a struggling child with oxygen mask, yours has to be in place first.

A Parent's Affirmation

Affirmations are bridges. They fill the gap between where you may be now to where you will be later in your thinking and believing. They are generally no good without a plan of action but you are holding and reading yours. I vouch for confidence as a foundation, but it will depend on where you are. You may feel like discipline or organization is next for study. Either way the affirmation will help you change your mindset if you say it out loud, remember— your ears are listening.

I have one of the greatest jobs on the planet! I don't need compensation, benefits, or credentials to do what I do. I am a parent. I am an overseer and steward of a life that was entrusted to me to replicate, teach, and direct in a safe and encouraging environment. I understand that my children will not always want to accept my help, my advice, or heed my warnings. Even so, I will not give up or back down when those trying times surface. I don't manipulate, abuse, or neglect my responsibility as a parent. Whether I am involved in their lives full or part time, all that matters is that I am present and available. I am a parent first and a friend later, trusting my instincts, discipline and guidance that are on the inside of me, learned through experience and filtered wisdom from others. I have a right to challenge, disrupt, and defend anything that goes against my role as a parent. I embrace this opportunity to be the most confident, effective, loving, and energetic parent for my children, because no one will ever love them like I do. They trust, believe in, and watch me, and I vow to be their standard.

Chapter Twelve – Confidence is for Individuality

I was a nervous wreck. I stood in a line of over 4,000, tall, beautiful, seemingly perfect, tan girls in Los Angeles, California. I remember telling my best friend Chelsea when we first pulled up to the line of about 10 people, "Oh hell naw, take me home, I don't belong here."

"What? You DO", she pleaded. "If no one else deserves a shot at this, you do. Look at all the preparation and everything you went through to get here. Even if you don't get picked, you were seen and judged and you need that."

Her sweet pep-talked turned into bold-faced seriousness. "Now, get out the car."

No sense in arguing with her. Besides the fact that we were already homeless, living in my Chrysler 300M, we had a flight later on that night which consisted of three different states and one lay-over. As newly trained flight attendants we couldn't afford to get a place of our own. We attempted to live in a crash pad with thirty-two other pilots and flight attendants, but when drama hit there, sleeping in the car was more peaceful. We signed up for a membership at a well-known gym so that we would have access to a hot shower. We washed our clothes and uniform at a laundromat and had the opportunity to eat out in every restaurant in California. We lived on Pacific Coast Highway, trying out the different beaches, going to parties and living care-free.

When one of us was called on a 3 or 4 day trip the other went along because we could fly for free. Only one flight attendant per jet, but even on the full passenger jets we were qualified to sit in the extra jump seat in the back, provided that we wore our uniform and offer to assist in the event of an emergency. That way when we had a layover in a city, we could actually sleep in a bed and not have to worry about paying for it. In some places like San Diego and New Jersey, it wasn't so bad. Then there were some that were in the middle of nowhere. Living out of my car was not only more convenient, but very common, we later found out.

When I saw the audition in the paper, my impulsive nature was ready to hit the runway. I had the confidence of a leopard and boldness of a lion. When we arrived, I forgot absolutely everything I learned about walking in heels and felt completely out of place. Because my best friend knew me and everything it took to get me to that very moment she was able to push me. Not because she wanted me to succeed, but because she did not want me to feel defeat.

I understood that.

When I was in middle school, I didn't see myself as pretty. My self-esteem was at an all-time low not just because of what the other kids said, but because what they said had caused me to create a prototype of what I should look like in order to be accepted. Creating a standard is very common practice in the mind of a child. It sort of goes like this:

Chapter Twelve – Confidence is for Individuality

"I'm ugly because I'm too dark, I wear thick glasses, I'm a little overweight and I'm not good enough to be a part of their clique. The common denominator in that clique is that no one is dark skinned, wear glasses, or is overweight. Because of that, I begin to think that those things are not acceptable when it has to do with being a part of something so I isolate myself based on that and I am led to believe that this is standard."

It doesn't just happen to children either. As a whole, our society always talks about "they". "They" say being thin is the only chance you have at being a model. "They" say that in order to be thin you have to be a vegetarian. "They" say that as a vegetarian you can't even eat fish, etc. I'm using this as an example because we tend to accept whatever is thrown at us and conform to it. Once we conform to it, we build our lives, practices, and families around it and it becomes our standard. Only the people who dare to go against the status-quo succeed beyond measure.

I didn't have a lot of confidence as a teenager. The only confidence that lived in me was my ability to disassociate. I didn't realize that there was a name for it at the time, but I have learned that the little girl who got good grades, played sports, and didn't rebel against her parents was not the same girl who went to sleep at night and dreamt of torturing the people who were hurting her. The only way to keep those two personas alive and in character was to keep them separate.

A little while after being released from the juvenile institution, I recognized the "beauty standard" in the world. It was all around me. I was exposed to things as an adult for the very first time. I was rough around the edges. As with anything else and based on my perception of the operation of life, if I needed it or needed to learn it, there was someone out there who had it, sold it, or taught it. I began my search for beauty schools. It was funny because I kept running into beauty products, cosmetology schools, and anything surface beauty could offer. Don't get me wrong, I needed all of that. I had never walked in a heel, wore makeup, put on a skirt, shaved my legs, or been in a position where I felt the need to do any of that. I learned very quickly about the power of femininity.

I finally stumbled upon a modeling school where the motto was to "be a model, or train to look like one". Sounded good to me. So for almost a year, I drove three hours every weekend to train. It was expensive and tiring, but this was my investment in me. The training was so intense that even if your original plan wasn't to pack up and move to New York, you sure felt like you wanted to with all of the confidence that was placed in you. For me it was Los Angeles. Mostly because of the weather, but also because I wanted to be more on the acting and commercial side of modeling, not so much the high fashion stiletto runway thing. It was appropriate because after I graduated from this modeling school, I went to work every day in a cubicle. I felt like I needed to utilize my new found confidence but the guys that I worked with and their advances and flattery did nothing for me.

One of my customers offered to fly me and a friend to the Mall of America in Minnesota. I had never flown, so I was definitely up for the trip. We weren't even 10, 000 feet in the air and I knew I wanted to be a flight attendant. They were stunning to me. The three on our plane were really nice and very well put together. Even though I enjoyed the flight and the destination, all I could think about was getting back home to research my new career.

I asked around about how to become a flight attendant and for the most part, people kept saying that you had to go to college, be a

Chapter Twelve – Confidence is for Individuality

pilot, and all sorts of ideas that were so far from true. I quickly learned that if I wanted to get to a position, I needed to seek those already in that position and follow their way until I held my own. So that's exactly what I did. Turns out, you have to be very friendly, customer focused, be able to fit in the jump seat and with or without heels reach the overhead bin and have enough confidence to keep people calm in the event of an emergency even if it meant your life was about to end.

Sounded easy enough to me....

Well, except for the last part.

But even that wasn't going to stop me. I got some training from a current flight attendant, received some do's and don'ts from another, joined a forum to find out who was hiring, and I was sent a free ticket to my first interview. It was a very good experience from start to finish.

I also found out that there were a whole lot of people during that time who wanted to be flight attendants. There were at least 400-500 interviewees who were invited as well. This was the time to execute my training from the modeling school and the advice from the senior flight attendants.

After we had a few interviews, group sessions, and a panel interview, I was on my way back home to Ohio. When I landed, I had a voicemail inviting me back for training as a flight attendant. I did it! I was picked! Amongst all those other people, they saw something different in me. That entire process instilled a heap of confidence in me and my ability to adapt. At the time, it had very little to do with how I looked on the outside apart from the professional dress for the interview. I was taught very early in my career training that whatever position I wanted, all I had to do was learn it, study it, act, and look like it at interview time. That is exactly what I did during the flight attendant interviews from the time I stepped into the airport until I landed back in Ohio.

I guess that confidence went into overflow when I decided to answer an audition call to be a "Deal or No Deal" Model for the television game show. As soon as we pulled up, I knew I was in over my head, but that didn't stop me. I made up in my mind that day that no matter what happens, I would take away something that I could use for the next time. When I was called to the area for evaluation, I was a nervous wreck. I knew I was put together on the outside by the way people stared at me when I walked into the room. That was my moment. For the first time ever, I didn't feel too dark, or too fat.

I didn't feel 'not good enough'.

That moment changed the inside of me because I did it afraid. I stepped out beyond my comfort zone to test my learning skills. The judges looked at me and most of them smiled and nodded with approval and I could feel the other contestants watching what they were saying. I didn't get picked that day. They said something along the lines of experience and that I was definitely gorgeous and should never give up on my aspirations of modeling.

I could've cried and been disappointed and maybe even depressed, but I wasn't. I was the complete opposite. You see, they did not say that I wasn't good enough, what they said was they were looking for more experience. What I heard was "keep on the same path. You will get your day. But today, for this thing, we are looking for different".

Chapter Twelve – Confidence is for Individuality

Sometimes it's how we take the words that are presented to us. This is why our communication is only five percent verbal- what is most understood is our non-verbal- our expressions, reactions and tone. I didn't care that I didn't get picked. I cared that they re-affirmed what I worked so hard to attain—beauty.

Some of you may feel like you want to step out into a dream career or venture but you allow what other people say that you lack, along with your own doubts to stop you from even taking a step in that direction.

Competence and confidence play well together. There are many definitions of competency. I created my own definition based on the original and added another based on my understanding of the word and my life experiences. Competency is an ability to learn a behavior or skill in the way and time that skill is needed. Because ability is a natural or acquired skill, it leaves the possibility open to anyone that is willing to put their natural skill to work or willing to acquire a new one and put it to work. Confidence is defined by a string of words that can only be executed with an action. Faith, belief, or trust in one's self or ability is my definition of confidence. Here is the fun part. Sometimes, you need to create enough confidence to walk into something requiring competence. From there, it's basically on-the-job training. I had never even flown before, let alone been responsible for so many people on that plane with me. However, I saw what it looked like, went after it, got an opportunity to learn it, learned it, and succeeded. If I would've allowed "them" to hold me back, that opportunity would've never existed for me. How many opportunities have you allowed someone else to talk you out of? It's time to revisit those opportunities and allow yourself to learn why you were drawn to them in the first place.

This time, you will be armed and ready with a one way ticket and a passport.

So please put on your seatbelt, and enjoy your flight.

Affirmations Continued

As I said earlier about parents, affirmations are a powerful tool for the re-training of the mind. As humans we simply talk too much and the closest thing to our mouth is our ears. Most of us destroy our chances before they present themselves simply by talking ourselves out of them. Affirmations, like the one I gave in the parents section, won't work if they are just thought about. Words only have power when spoken. In your mind they are only thoughts and when you don't give birth to thoughts, they die or get buried. So before we move forward, go back to the affirmation, add or take away what you need to make it fit for you and then say it aloud.

Whether you are striving to become an entrepreneur, a better parent, or the best "you" you can be, this is where it has to start. Just by reading this book you have begun a journey worth a thousand trips. You will be surprised at how you grow and change just by allowing yourself to be open to the tools that I teach you. Most of what I learned was learned the hard way- usually after hitting rock bottom, being taken advantage of, or just feeling both inadequate and frustrated because of that feeling of inadequacy based on historical events in my life. It's time to shorten your learning curve by teaching you from the deepest layer of your foundation all the way to the surface of your identity how to love who you are, appreciate what you have been though that makes you who you are, and how to revamp that into a tangible reflection in the mirror.

Chapter Twelve – Confidence is for Individuality

The hardest part is getting started. Fully understanding that you need this, that you want this and that it will change your life is enough to completely make you change your mind or draw back.

In her book *A Return to Love*, Marianne Williamson says:

"...Our deepest fear is not that we are inadequate. Our deepest fear is that we are powerful beyond measure. It is our light, not our darkness that most frightens us. We ask ourselves, who am I to be brilliant, gorgeous, talented, and fabulous? Actually, who are you not to be? You are a child of God. Your playing small does not serve the world. There is nothing enlightened about shrinking so that other people won't feel insecure around you. We are all meant to shine, as children do. We were born to make manifest the glory of God that is within us. It's not just in some of us; it's in everyone. And as we let our own light shine, we unconsciously give other people permission to do the same. As we are liberated from our own fear, our presence automatically liberates others."

This is as true to your soul as you allow it to be. As you begin to rebuild your thoughts and actions while implementing new strategies and possibilities you will also learn how to automatically filter those things that do not agree with your morale, character, or vision. This is a process that very few learn to grasp. The filtering process alone will also stand in as a boundary setter and a time management tool. Both of these are crucial on your journey.

Leadership Unleashed

As an individual, confidence has extraordinary power. An individual with confidence exemplifies confidence in all of their roles. Maybe not all of them all of the time, but it will definitely be evident. For most of us, it's not satisfying to just a have a job that we go to everyday. We need to feel like we are making a difference. Even though most of the time financial success may come from that, it is not the financial success that we expect or depend on, it is the feeling of knowing that we are a small part of a bigger picture and changing the world accordingly.

Most of these types of individuals operate in this order:

1. Discover a better way
2. Fight against opposition
3. Make and declare their stand
4. Become a life student of that better way
5. Receive a mass following based on all of the above

It may not happen exactly that way for all of them, but the possibility is present in their lives and also in the people who believe in them.

I call these people "fight back leaders". There is never one sure fire way to do something to achieve an end result, but the process can be made easier or harder depending on whether or not the trainee surrounds themselves with the right support system. If you believe that your support system has to be people you know personally, you are wrong. You can accept and learn from a leader and never sit at a table with them or meet them in person. I call them "fight back leaders" because what they represent goes against what is considered the norm most of the time. They don't need brand marketing or advertising because their brand is personal and purposeful. People will always seek out what they need and fight back leaders are there

Chapter Twelve – Confidence is for Individuality

to offer a new idea, way of thinking, or introduce a new concept or flow of process. This particular elite group has built their empires on their beliefs. And frankly, those wouldn't be sustained if they weren't getting results, right?

If you were interested in getting rich, would you take advice from a store manager who is having issues with money management, or would you rather learn from a millionaire who offers an online course to get you started on your path. Whether or not the second option is a risk is irrelevant. The point is, who would you rather learn from?

I'm going to introduce you to a few of the members of my personal "mastermind" group. These are people that I study under, have learned from, and whose teaching has changed my life in a profound way. You are more than welcome to start with mine—depending on what you need. You can also create your own based on your goals and aspirations. Keep in mind that everyone learns differently and just because the reception is different doesn't make the message right or wrong.

David "Avocado" Wolfe—"The Raw Food Extroindaire" aka "The Rock Star of the Super foods and Longevity World" is fiercely being sought after by everyone from multi-millionaires to single moms for healthier foods and lifestyles so they can live longer and feel better. He equipped me to fight back against disease and this diet fad that is driving people up the wall, sending them into depression and causing them to have feelings of inadequacy, leading them to hop from diet to diet giving a maximum effort and receiving no results, when really all they have to do is eat kale. (I'm being ornery with that last statement, but it's that simple)

Joyce Meyer, founder of a Christian non-profit organization that teaches, instructs and whips Christians into shape while feeding the hungry and delivering the Gospel all around the world. Most of my biblical training and strengthening came from sitting under her ministry. I read, listen, learn, and implement her strategies that have brought an extreme change to my life and those around me. Most people think she is just a televangelist. She equipped me with the spiritual fearless "fight back" mentality by yelling at me to "DO IT AFRAID" through the TV. She is also the reason why I have some of the confidence I do, one of the most important being the confidence to forgive. I am a Christian and I believe in God. My relationship with Him has grown over the years. If you can picture this, He is in the heavens overseeing the earth and everyone's path. Because everyone's path is unique and purposeful, He has overseers directing traffic showing them the way so they don't end up on a wrong path. She did that for me spiritually. She was able to have such an impact on me because her years of sexual abuse by her father didn't keep her from her original purpose and design and helps define who she is. She has bestowed that upon me.

Brendon Burchard, founder of Experts Academy and author of <u>The Millionaire Messenger</u>. He is responsible for teaching me how to implement and reach others with my message. My business model is a replica of his (with a few changes to fit my own personality, of course). Brendon gave me permission to take my creativity, desire to help others, and dubbed me an "expert" in a practical, tactful, and meaningful way. I owe the completion of this book to him for yelling at me through my cd player to "get off my butt" and get it done, because basically people are failing because I'm not in my proper place in this world helping people with what I know. He has equipped me with the "fight back" of self-defeat. Even though the

Chapter Twelve – Confidence is for Individuality

events in my life clearly point toward purpose, I used to feel very unrefined half of the time and over-intelligent the other half. Under his instruction I am an "Entrepreneurial Expert". I tried to attend various colleges from the time I left the institution at 21 until I was about 32 but I had to learn life, and trying to learn the basics of life on top of homework and midterms felt like torture, so I never finished. None of the majors fit my purpose and I actually lived some of the case studies the students were learning about and I grew bored. Brendan inspired me and taught me that I do have a right to share my message and make money while doing so. Goodbye welfare, hello entrepreneurship. I call his program my PhD in a box.

James Colquhoun and Laurentine ten Bosch, the directors of the award winning documentaries "Food Matters" and "Hungry for Change" completely revamped my view on today's food system and taught me how to eat to live. Because I grew up in a correctional system and was then handed off to a government system, I was ignorant to a lot of dos and don'ts to that the general population knows about food. Most people who choose to eat the wrong stuff or choose to pop a pill for every ill are doing so out of choice knowing there is an alternative. My struggle was that I did not know there was one. Therefore, if I had a headache, I would pop a couple pills, wash it down with some high fructose corn syrup and order a number 5 at the drive thru because I felt better but hungry an hour later. They have equipped me with the "fight back" against chronic disease and depression by showing me that if I have no other control on the face of the planet, I can control what I put in my mouth and that the best way the win the fight against cancers and other chronic illnesses is simply to not to get in the ring. They have probably saved me millions of dollars, unnecessary hospital visits and, oh, did I mention, my life! Because of their philosophy, I am in my late thirties, have three kids, black, and have never been diagnosed with any chronic illness. I am in great shape, have an athletic physique, and an energy level out of this world.

No diets.

Ever.

Marci Sutherland, the previous Superintendent at the Ohio Department of Youth Services, is not just a wake up, go to work, do the job, go home, corporate power junkie. As the overseer of thousands of at-risk youth, I probably spent the majority of my life under her instruction. She took the time to counsel me, teach me, lead me, correct me, and filled my mental box with everything she could to prepare me to live in a society, that to me, was like an entirely different planet. Her ability to meet me where I was in my life as a young teenager and guide me into adulthood continues to astonish me to this day. Because I did not have my mom as I was growing up inside the walls of the institution, she became that for me, in a way that was ethical for her and extremely beneficial to and for me. She did not allow me to become a system experiment. Medicine-pushing psychiatrists couldn't touch me, hatred-filled family members could not visit me. She understood very well that our youth are in trouble. They have no advocate outside of the parents that sell them off to sexual slavery. They are bound by teachers and coaches who manipulate, rape, and take advantage of the children in their care. It is because of people like her who are still passionate and sincere about their calling that I have the character and mental strength of a lioness. She equipped me my "fight back" as a parent.

Dr. David C. Forbes Jr. and Dr. Tracy Forbes, the founders of Ever Increasing Life Ministries located in Columbus, Ohio, are my

Chapter Twelve – Confidence is for Individuality

"home". Home is a place where you feel safe. It is a place where you are free to be who you are no matter how many times it changes. At home, you have the freedom to grow, learn, step out, make mistakes, come back, learn again, step out, make more mistakes, come back, and maneuver in that process no matter how many times or how long it takes. If you ever feel threatened, unsure, or ill-prepared, home is a place you can come back to and learn the process again. You can't Google home because home is filtered. Your morals, values, and perceptions are created here. In that sense, when you step out into the world with all of its opinions, tactics, and beliefs you don't have to go with the wind.

Home is where the saying lives "If you don't stand for something, you will fall for anything". Lastly, home is filled with unconditional love. A love that doesn't change based on your performance or your ability (or lack of) to return its value. Love which is safe enough to allow anger and encouraged to forgive. A love that corrects and disciplines, but uses manipulation or allows embarrassment. This is where I was trained up and fully equipped to be a woman, wife, mom, leader, and friend. I didn't have a place to go when I was released from the system at twenty-one, aside from my one bedroom apartment. Although I had the opportunity to participate in this ministry at seventeen, its full value came into effect not when I attended church services on Sunday, but when I got plugged in to the "community" of the church. I allowed people to get to know me and I them. I participated as a servant and eventually became a leader of a small circle or group. I went through one year of ministry training and actually began to implement what I was learning.

When I departed at thirty, everything I learned became of value to my life and surroundings. I was amazed. One of the most valuable lessons in my entire adult life as a woman in leadership in any entity is, "You must first learn to follow, before you can lead".

This is part of *my* leadership team. I have a results expert for every area of my life. These are people that I learn from continually. Some of them know me personally, some do not, but I don't need to know them personally to adapt their methods and philosophies in my journey. They display confidence in their personality and expertise in their field.

The same goes for you.

Personal development is a lifelong process. As with life in general there are seasons in which we learn to adapt, accept the lessons of that particular season and move forward repeating the process with the next season. For me, winter was the worst season ever. In fact, I disliked snow so much that I subconsciously and literally moved south every time winter came for a few years straight. Seasons involve more than weather changes. There is wisdom and metaphoric lessons to be learned when we embrace each one. I have grown to appreciate the winter because it symbolizes a deep change in structure. This is the only season where things freeze. The drop in temperature kills off old matter like insects and viruses etc. The blankets of pure white snow are beautiful during that process. Underneath those blankets of snow, transition is taking place so that when it melts, the ice becomes water and aids in the new growth process of spring. This analogy has been a deep personal experience for me and embracing the winter season has changed my life.

What season of your life do you need to embrace? Whatever that season may be, always keep in mind that it will change. What is most comforting is that once you began this path in restoring and

Chapter Twelve – Confidence is for Individuality

re-building your confidence, seasons will not only become clear, but desired.

Re-building the confidence that we may have never known or taking back the confidence that was stolen from us through the mistakes and failures of others is the one most ignored or forgotten aspects of ourselves and our personal development and needs to be addressed. We draw from life, create prejudices, learn malfunctions, run into disorder, can't recognize the dysfunction, are unable to set boundaries, and can relinquish our right to re-learn all of those above because of other people and the influence they have in our lives. These people are our parents, spouses, other family, and friends. While they may not intentionally mean to do harm, it doesn't change the fact that harm is done. Now, we have the ability to undo that harm.

The Decision

It all starts with a decision.

Let's use Kathy's story as an example. Kathy is a smart driven young woman. She is a very quick learner and essentially can apply for and receive any job in her marketing field. Her IQ is very high and she is well-versed in any program that has to do with an office or marketing, so she can score off the charts with no problem. On paper, Kathy has it made. When she is called in for an interview, that she quickly gets because of her resume and scores, but she fails miserably. She has a hard time with confidence and communication, especially with men, who are typically her interviewers. The executives feel that if Kathy has a hard time in an interview, how will she market their product all around the world? Kathy knows that it's always the interview that she fails. She gets pretty down on herself and eventually just settles for a cubicle job where the only requirement is being polite and customer-oriented. She isn't happy at all, but she will go on to work there for years with all of her raw talent unused and continue operating in a pay grade a lot lower than she had hoped to be in at this stage in her life.

Kathy was severely sexually abused by her father during her entire childhood. She tried to tell her mom once during her middle school years, but her mom told her she was exaggerating and shouldn't say things about people that are not true. This caused Kathy not to go into any further details with her mom and caused her to have extremely low self-esteem. Kathy threw herself into her studies and went on to graduate at the top of her class. She never mentioned the abuse again. It eventually stopped once she graduated and moved into her own place, but Kathy's memories of it will not stop. Her father threatened her, intimidated her, and bullied her with his words and authority. Every time she sees him, she is reminded of his abuse, but she doesn't want to give up her relationship with her mom, so she continues to visit.

Kathy hasn't put the two together yet, but her abuse from her father has caused severe self-esteem issues in her as a woman. This is why she has a hard time with male authority and with her own confidence when it really counts. Kathy will need to find a way to conquer this issue by going back, confronting, and forgiving her past and regaining her confidence. If she doesn't, it's not that her life will be completely miserable; however, she will never reach her true potential and value her true worth until she faces this issue. If Kathy has a daughter, she will unconsciously pass her lack of confidence issues onto her daughter because her daughter will watch and learn from her. This cycle will continue until a decision is made to stop it, and it's interrupted and figured out. With all of the self-help and materials available, it is likely that her daughter will be curious and

Chapter Twelve – Confidence is for Individuality

want to learn more. That will depend on how her daughter views the world and her place in it. It will all depend on the decision of that individual to change.

The new reality or trend in a learning environment is completely free and open to interpretation without judgment or previous experience. Life and learning are both strategic and subjective. In life, the strategy is often unreachable even though it may make sense to the mind. Strategy says if we can change what has happened to us in our past then we wouldn't be where we are now. Unfortunately, we can't go back. Life is subjective because it belongs to us individually. Those of you who have had a great life may not want to change it so that it produces different results, but instead, be able to better relate to the struggles of others to be able to share your successes to them. The common denominator is that whether life in our past was phenomenal or shitty, we will always want to change it in some form based on where we are now.

The new trend in learning is the same way. You are expected to be able to take in new information, process it quickly, and apply it immediately.

Strategically, there is a systematic way to learn a skill or trade. Subjectively, how you learn that skill or trade will be based on how you learn period. For instance, I am a vision audible and tactful learner, therefore, if I want to learn photography, I won't do so well in a traditional setting where I have to learn the history of the lens, acquire the knowledge of color, and appreciate the value of the history of the camera. I wouldn't make it. Instead, I will purchase the camera, read the instructions so I don't damage it, explore it's functions, have fun with it, then go to YouTube and find a training video listen to what they say don't do, do what they say to do and spend a week or so creating pictures. The ones that come out wrong, I figure out why and re-take and the ones that come out perfect, I keep taking ones like them. Now, how many times do you think someone who views my photographs will be amazed at the ones that I thought came out wrong? Are you with me? Most of us love to learn in that way.

We embrace the challenge and appreciate the time it takes to learn it.

We have an idea, we visualize it, collect the necessary elements to build it and we go for it. If we fail then that idea dies or we try a different one. We do this in every area of our life all the time. With the technology of today, failing isn't even possible but failing to try is. Those who never take an idea from visualization to implementation are bored with life and can't wait to check out. Those of us who at least step out and try to implement an idea make room for more experiences and higher learning. We master the art of learning in its most effective form: trial and error.

It *is* possible for you to start that business, A'ce that interview, be that parent that your kids bring their kids back to for advice, be that sexy wife that your husband desires, be the husband that your wife can brag about, and manage your children so they obey and respect you—without duct tape and a time-out chair.

I'm going to teach you how to allow confidence into your life by breaking down old walls and building new ones. I, too, was tired of people telling me what I am and am not capable of based on their perceptions, which meant less than a bowl of nuts at a bar. I'm going to show you how to take your past and make it work in your favor stepping out of the victim mentality where most of you

Chapter Twelve – Confidence is for Individuality

have taken up residence. I want to make you laugh with sarcastic side comments and writing things in black and white that most people won't say in public and touch your heart with stories and experiences that seem too harsh to share.

Eliminate the Extras

During your journey people will automatically latch themselves onto you. It seems like Jesus knew this during His ministry and used the process of elimination based on who stuck around when the going got tough. We can take advantage of this same process when we go through a wilderness trip.

Wilderness trips are designed to condition you. Hardship will happen. Obstacles will get in the way and life will certainly take you off the main path for a season. Wilderness trips never come with warning signs, orange cones or caution tape. You are not guaranteed a partner, service dog, or Purple Heart and only you can decide what to make of the journey.

You will face affliction. Along with the Negative-Nellies and Nay-Sayers you will encounter challenges within the processes of this book that will make you second guess your journey. People will tell you that this training is ridiculous and unnecessary. Even after the change in you is obvious and you are thriving, other people will still have a better idea for you, more that you can do and other things you can change. I am here to confirm that you will never meet the expectations of people. In fact you will find that weeding is necessary and refreshing.

Eliminating extras begin with the people in your life who refuse to allow you room to grow. They are controlling, manipulative, and don't accept you for who really you are. They never encourage your natural gifts and abilities but are more than willing to point out your flaws and present stumbles and no, I'm not *just* talking about your Mother-in-Law. These people are always in your face but rarely have anything to positive to say. You can chat with them all day about big city housewives or YouTube sensations, but if you mention a goal or a dream, you're killing the mood.

There are also "side trackers"—you know those who encourage you to fulfill their dream because they never did. Everything you do must be done according to their standards because it satisfies their expectation of who they think you should be. With these people, you are encouraged to dream–but only at night, preferably Tuesdays and they will set the alarm for you to awaken. No, I'm not *just* talking about your parents.

It's time to get these people and their opinions out of your face and into the back row seat of your movie premier. It doesn't matter who they are or if they mean well, they will need to earn a place in your vision. Most of the time, we lack confidence because of the "I-didn't-mean-it-that-way" opinion of others. Along with subliminal messages, endless selfies and status updates, it's a wonder we still use our full birth "instagooglintubetwitface" names. We forget that we have a responsibility to raise another generation. Life evolves and doesn't just end here and we are not just losing time, we are wasting it.

When we die and our tombstone is created, it will have two vital pieces of information:

Our birth date – Our death date

Chapter Twelve – Confidence is for Individuality

Unfortunately, the one, small hyphen in between those dates represents the total summary of our accomplishments, legacies, and experiences. The only thing that continues to live on is what we have given away to others in the form of stories, advice, principles, and rites of passage. We have become so selfish and self-focused in today's modern society that we have a hard time seeing past our own limitations, limiting our ability to reach out. What's worse is that we then stop looking for a reason to share those life lessons, we inadvertently withhold vital information that could save a life, heal a body, or mend a broken relationship.

You are the BEST Credential

I don't knock traditional education. Some of you have three degrees, two certificates, and a scholarship to keep going. You will learn and study to your hearts content, discover that breakthrough formula that reverses sickness and lead your country into financial freedom. I commend you. You value instruction, you submit to structure, and you have crazy-cool focus. You have a clear and dedicated purpose. Without people like you, the world would revolve around Adderall.

For those of you who may have raised your hands, at five, on the carpet at circle time in preschool and declared your career and degrees but were interrupted by life's lemons, your purpose is equally clear and intentional. How? Because while concentrated careers offer a detailed blueprint in instruction and direction, life and it's many seasons do not. Some of you dreamed of or started out on that path but was interrupted by marriage, children, and all the stuff that holds it together. Some of you fell into a ditch on that path and were injured by abuse, homelessness, sickness, or disease. Some of you have even experienced pain through the death of someone close and have a desire to share their wisdom. The remainders of you have just figured out an easier, more effective way of doing or becoming something but you have no confidence to share that experience with other people. You too, have a dedicated purpose. It may not be as clear as raw talent, but it does exist.

Brendon Burchard, author of *The Millionaire Messenger* puts it in a way that resonated with my passion and desire to step out. He says,

"…I deeply believe it is part of our life's purpose to learn and experience the world and then turn and lend a hand to others who are also trying to get ahead. If you have struggled through something and survived, you should help those now struggling. If you have achieved the impossible, make it possible for others to achieve the same. If you have spent years figuring something out, why not shorten someone else's learning curve? If you have cracked the code to success in any area, why not give everyone the secret?"

This statement validated my belief that our lives and experiences are not just for us-they are for other people. We just need to get out of our own way.

We are over-educated, misunderstood, and beyond qualified.

The Snapshot of a Confident Individual:

1. A confident individual will not feel the need to be everybody's everything. They can and will create boundaries, know when to say no, and not feel bad about letting others feel disappointed when they do. This is a practice that will take time and effort and will need to be practiced in order to grow in strength and competence.

Chapter Twelve – Confidence is for Individuality

2. A confident individual has no opinion where they have no responsibility. There is no need for a confident person to gossip, put another person down or engage in conversation where they do not have the authority or ability to be or offer a direct result.

3. Confident individuals choose and chew their words very carefully as not to offend or choke. When they believe to have said something wrong or offensive a confident individual can return to the person or group and apologize without making excuses. Confident people learn very quickly that their immediate surroundings, world, and families are affected by their words and they have power to build or break.

4. A confident individual does not see a color of skin, but rather a content of character. They judge people carefully and filter them appropriately. They don't keep company with negative people and don't allow negative people to speak into their lives or business.

5. A confident person is a lifelong listener. They are able to listen with their minds, hearts and surroundings. They are able to take in information as it comes and filter what is needed and set aside what is not. They are slow to tell other people what they should do and instead offer guidance and support when requested.

Men and women of confidence, here is to your Alternative Upgrade to Me 2.0, the new system that everyone expects you to have, but can't teach you how to download it. I commend and support you through your journey of purposeful trial and error into your completion of your new found sense of purpose and fulfillment.

First, say this affirmation out loud, then, grab your latte and let's move.

Individual affirmation for men:

I am a man. I am courageous, I am strong and I am a leader. My career, hobbies and personality does not change the badge of my birthright. I have gone through hard times but my battlefield is also my training ground. It doesn't always look good, but that doesn't change the victory ahead. I have been through wars of many types, some in my home, and some in my mind. I have suffered and I have caused suffering. I have fought, hid, lost hope, and hit rock bottom several times. Today, I call out to the man on the inside of me that won't allow me to quit. The masculine qualities that society, religion, and bad relationships tried to take from me will no longer have access to the fire in my heart. Today, I make a decision to change what needs to be changed in my life to make me happier and more fulfilled.

Whether it's my weight, my career, my time or my parenting, I declare that today is my breaking ground day. What I have done, been through, or been scared by will never determine who I am or what I become. I am the only me with my fingerprint in the entire universe which means that what I have to offer my family, my job, my friends, my community, and myself cannot be copied or created by anyone other than me. From this day forward, I will embrace life and accept me as I am. I will make revision along the way that will compliment my nature and not destroy it. I am a confident man who will lead our sons and daughters by an example so excellent that they will not be able to hear what I say because they are intently watching how I live.

Chapter Twelve – Confidence is for Individuality

Individual affirmation for women:

I am amazing. I am beautiful. I am confident. My career, family, relationships and hobbies do not change the imprint on my heart. I am exactly where I am supposed to be in this world. My battlefield is also my training ground and it doesn't always feel good, but that doesn't change the victory ahead. I have been through bad and good experiences, I have suffered and I have caused suffering. I have fought, cried, lost hope, and hit rock bottom several times.

Today, I call out to the woman on the inside of me that won't allow me to quit. The feminine power of my ideas and visions will no longer take a backseat to my fears and insecurities.

Today, I make a decision to change what needs to be changed in my life to make me happier and more fulfilled. Whether it's my weight, hair color, my career, or my parenting, I declare that today is my breaking ground day. What I have done, been through, or been hurt by will never determine who I am or what I become. I am the only me with my fingerprint in the entire universe which means that what I have to offer my family, my job, my friends, my community and myself cannot be copied or created by anyone other than me. From this day forward, I will embrace life and accept me as I am. I will create and define my own version of feminine power and use it to better the world around me. I am a confident woman who will lead our sons and daughters by an example so excellent that they will not be able to hear what I say because they are intently watching how I live.

Chapter Thirteen – Confidence is for Relationships

When I met you

I liked you

When I liked you

I loved you

When I loved you

I let you

When I let you

I lost you

When I lost you

I died.

The Revelation of Heartbreak

I stood under the steamy hot shower as it covered me from head to toe. Each trickle that came together caused a stream that blanketed me and traveled through my hair, down my back, and covered me entirely before streaming down the drain. The strokes of water and temperature of the heat comforted and calmed my soul. Under the pure embrace of the water, I felt cared for, soothed, and relieved. With blurred vision, I watched the water make its way down the drain. It didn't linger or hesitate, something I wished pain wouldn't do either. I couldn't tell the difference between the water and my tears because they merged together so seamlessly and left so quickly. My heart clattered with the sound of the water that drowned out the cry that softly hummed its way out of my body. The warm mist encased every inch of my body and seemed to affirm what I needed at that very moment. What every woman needs.

A covering.

He immediately had my attention when he walked into the room. There was no introduction. I didn't need to know his name or engage in a conversation with him. I didn't desire his love and I was definitely not in a position to begin dating. This attraction lingered so far beyond an emotional feeling that I had to catch myself physically from floating away. I didn't know what had captured me and why it did so suddenly and freely. From that moment on, I believed in love at first sight and had never met such an untimely beautiful disaster.

I could've lived on that feeling alone—never knowing his name. I was certain that that's how it would be.

Chapter Thirteen – Confidence is for Relationships

His eyes locked with mine. At that inconvenient moment, there was no turning back; I knew he felt the exact same thing I did. He smiled at me. I melted like the chocolate coating of a nutty M&M.

He was definitely gorgeous to me, but what connected us was so far beyond physical that there were no words. Trust me. If there were words out there to describe what happened to me in that moment on that day, I would've found them by now, given them to my editor and put every romantic novel to shame. The words never came, only the friendship.

Whatever was awakened in me that day arose from the inner core of my soul and it was a presence that would never return to its slumber. I knew that he could never do wrong in my eyes because I would choose to only see his heart not his flaws. I knew that I would, without hesitation, forgive him for every wrong that he would ever do. This man would always have my understanding and my loyalty whether we remained friends or not. I immediately handed my heart over to him knowing that he could break it, but hoping he wouldn't. Everything on the inside of him reached in and grabbed everything on the inside of me. Whatever he had to offer, I would take it and be all that he needed in return. I never been inside of love like that before; head spinning, non-resistance and full expression of emotion without my initiation. It wasn't obvious to the human eye. It wasn't expressed until later. All of the emotions I just described took place on the inside of me. I wondered if this was the gift that God meant for us to feel in the way He felt for us:

True, untainted, imperfect, raw, heartfelt, and sacrificial love.

I needed that.

I had just came through what I believe for me was rock bottom since I had been home. I had been homeless for six months and scrambling to feed my kids because I traveled across the country for a job that I thought was a perfect fit for me as a new graduate but turned out to be not-so-perfect, discriminatory, and unethical.

My self-esteem plummeted and I felt like drama was on the horizon. The remarkable thing about hitting rock bottom, though, is that there is only one direction left to look.

Up.

That's exactly what I did. This was my spiritual epiphany. This is when my flaky on and off religion with God was forming into a beautiful mature relationship. I had gone to church for years doing what I was told, following all the rules, not doing this, trying to do that, until I became exhausted and miserable. I had to be a perfect church girl because I didn't have any pardons left. I pictured God saying to me that since He has forgiven me for the worst thing possible, I could never mess up again.

I learned how untrue and ridiculous that was when God revealed His true love for me by grace. I felt such a relief, that I cried nonstop for two weeks. I'd finally let go of my own idea of how I should be and I allowed the love of Jesus to teach and form me. I was tired of running from my calling. I connected the dots from my life up to that point and everything I had learned up to that moment was for that moment.

My confidence returned and my heart grew soft toward others. I was surrounded by deeper understanding, unmovable strength, and extreme levels of intelligence.

Chapter Thirteen – Confidence is for Relationships

I was also surrounded by cockroaches at the homeless shelter, so I knew it was time to make moves and get myself together, yeah, I knew that I had a job to do. I didn't have the luxury of self-pity and woe-is-me mentality. Perseverance was too heavy in my lungs and I felt stronger than I had ever felt before. Every emotion was heightened, every color was brighter and I even became passionate about the life that was unexpectedly growing on the inside of me. I was at peace, I was ok. I made a covenant with myself that I would not allow anything else to pull me off my path. Not depression, low self-esteem, love...

And definitely not a broken heart.

For the first time in my life, I had chosen love. I cared for him deeply. I was the best friend to him that I wished someone was to me. I had given him a place in my life that he hadn't earned or deserved. I paid for that. His love came with secrets, lies, and manipulation. I still chose to forgive and love him. When the time came for him to choose, he didn't. Until it was too late. It was no longer love, it had become unhealthy.

I was so taken by the intensity of feeling that replaced what I thought was love on the inside of me. It was commanding, strong and

Permanent.

The heart I thought was mine was ripped out of my chest with no warning or mercy. The circulation of fondness that belonged to me was replaced by thick, heavy, lingering smog. As I stood underneath the shower that day, my tears were understood and necessary.

I cried for what I had.

I cried for what I wanted.

I cried for what I'd lost.

As the water covered me, it was as if it cleansed and convinced me that being open to such a powerful emotion as love would allow me to love again. The steaming hot shower covered me from head to toe and I submitted to its healing power. I made an agreement with my soul that I would allow love to capture me again one day. The water sealed the agreement when it diluted my tears and mended my broken heart.

I knew for a fact that I would never feel that way again. I knew that that feeling was so rare because it chose me. I was wrong. As soon as I decided to step out of the whirlwind of "feeling" and let that go, love did happen again. Because love is what you were designed with, you never have to stay in something that is unhealthy out of fear. Fear has no measure against love. People die for love and run from fear.

When I met the person that took the fear away and challenged me to come up higher, I grew fond of him. That fondness turned into appreciation. That appreciation turned into respect. The respect turned into friendship and that's how love came back. The difference was, I chose it. Everyone we meet won't be in an equal stage of life. When we have a foundation of confidence, people who need that missing piece will be attracted to it. At that point, the love that kind of hangs out on the inside of you grows stronger and wiser. Then you will get to choose who to give that gift to. Someone who deserves it. It is a gift alone to want to pour love into someone who you *know* will embrace, respect, and protect it with their life. I don't even have a strong desire to let him know because he too has a choice on whether or not to receive it. Yes, there is more power in decision than there is in feeling.

Chapter Thirteen – Confidence is for Relationships

To be in a position to be able to offer that love is a gift. I fell in love with love and I will never be the same. I now value the only lesson I need about love and that is:

Because I fully accept, embrace and love myself, I can truly love another. For at the foundation of love itself is complete and uninhibited

Selflessness.

Relationships are the number one human need besides water and food. God gave Adam Eve. Whether your faith includes biblical ideas or not, the principle is foundation, there is no other example and will always be the same. I am of the Christian Faith so I will use this biblical reference as an example of how things have changed so much and how we have either adapted to those changes with the true foundation still lurking around in our hearts, or life has done so much damage in us that we refuse to see anything new outside of our own experiences and understanding. Once we figure out which it is we will know exactly what to do.

Throughout the Bible, the men that marry picked their wives and married them immediately. There were no movie trips, flower arrangements, or candle lit dinners anywhere for the taking. In some instances the men had to prove they were worthy through strength and battle and in other instances the women had to use the power of feminine seduction. Courtship was non-existent. However, those unions were sacred and safe for both the man and the woman. Those unions lasted a lifetime.

Fast forward to this year and our men are battling sexuality, pornography, and financial stress. Our women are forced into unrealistic molds and expectations against flawless beauty and false advertisement in what that beauty should look like. Girls who are to one day become women of virtue, leadership, and admiration are being solicited and sold as sexual slaves before the age of seven. Billboards are filled with sexual solicitation, not from real beautiful women, but airbrushed and starving ones. Then our husbands want us to look and act like that false description of "sexy".

Women are damaging their own families by trying to trap and manipulate men. We get pregnant by men thinking that's the only way to make them stay. Then, we trap them and threaten to keep the children from their fathers if they want to leave the relationship. Or refuse to allow visitation until payments are made. As a result of this, men are losing their confidence and God given masculinity and no longer have a desire to fight for their families.

They may stick around for their kids, but they will grab on to the first woman that offers them more or builds them up and never remain faithful. The kids suffer because the love between mom and dad is so gone that arguing and fighting replaces love and affection. The man's mental health wiring gets tangled up so much so that shooting everyone in the house, themselves included, appears to be the only way out of the trap we set. I'm not judging because I used to be one of those women who thought that way. I changed my mentality, increased my confidence, and now realize that I am a privilege, not certainty. I allow love to be free, including free to choose me. Anything else is abuse.

The nature of abusive relationships has always been around and, like bullying, is not new. Abusers are the same; they just have new vehicles in which to operate. Being confident in a relationship doesn't happen immediately upon entering into one. The foundation of being a confident *individual* has to be there first.

Chapter Thirteen – Confidence is for Relationships

The old saying is, I bring 50% and you bring 50% and together—we will be 100%.

Unfortunately, this equation only works with tangible material and not the human spirit. The new goal is both individuals bringing to the table the absolute best 100% they can so that the combination will always be over 100% and have room to grow into 200%. If I have lost you at this point I'll simplify by saying this:

No one individual on the face of this earth is a standard. We are all so different that no two fingerprints are alike. As we go through life and develop relationships, we have to allow each person to freely be themselves. Their life experiences, hopes, dreams, ideas and emotions were different from the womb until death and will never have a duplicate. Therefore, we have to train ourselves to have this understanding with each and every individual we allow into our lives. They will not think like we do nor will they feel emotions in the same way we do. Their thought processes and personalities have been shaped from their life as an individual. When they enter our world, they are bringing themselves and we have no right to try and alter, change, or seemingly improve who they are because there is no standard or model that they *need* to become.

Confidence in a relationship requires a lot of risk and little understanding. We don't always need to understand why a person is the way they are. What we need to ask ourselves is can this individual add value to my life or can I add value to theirs. It is a servant's attitude that creates and holds together the best relationships as we learn from each other while continuing to grow on our own.

We run into three main issues that causes us to have problematic relationships that destroy self-esteem and they are:

1. **Manipulation.** Selfishness is a relationship destroyer before anything else. The focus isn't on the relationship during selfishness, it's on the individual. We attempt to train that individual to think and be like we are so that they are more manageable. We have a hard time accepting their best 100%. Deeper issues involving manipulation includes divorce and manipulation with children because one party in the relationship is having a hard time moving on. Another issue is not allowing a child to have a relationship with the other parent based on personal feeling about them or bitterness left behind in the old relationship. Don't get me wrong, there are instances where the other parent could do more harm than good. It is then up to the parent taking care of the child to protect that child. I know about this firsthand.

2. **Lack of Boundaries.** Every relationship needs a set of boundaries that can only be established during the relationship. When there are no boundaries the relationship turns problematic and most of the time abusive. Most people don't even believe they are in an abusive relationship because they have become accustomed to the behaviors in that relationship for so long. So many of our young people go through this right now because technology never sleeps and they are so inexperienced that they don't realize when someone is attempting to control them due to lack of boundaries.

3. **Lack of healthy esteem as an individual.** As I stated earlier, the number one characteristic of a true healthy and confident person is selflessness. It is the selflessness that is able to put a child's needs before our own. That same selflessness can forgive and forget easily because it chooses to celebrate the best

Chapter Thirteen – Confidence is for Relationships

of the other person and not the worst. Also, when we don't know, love, or accept ourselves, we conform to every relationship we are ever a part of and each time that relationship ends and we enter another, we become a vicious cycle of everyone else. Our individuality get so buried deep that when we are really ready to show the world our individuality, we either don't know or haven't accepted who that is. It's draining.

We learn from each other even when we don't realize it. This is all a part of the process of becoming our best 100%. What we are not learning by accident we need to learn on purpose. It is said that more second marriages last longer than firsts. I'm not sure how statistically true that is, but I can definitely see the logic because when I got married the first time I had no clue. I thought I would magically turn into Betty Crocker and be dubbed soccer mom. I learned very quickly that Betty Crocker is a brand more so than a person and that I enjoy cooking her items more than trying to duplicate the character. I very quickly learned that soccer mom is not something to volunteer for and that snack mom is better. I basically came to the conclusion that if I want to have a better second marriage than I had better get around and under marriages that are in elite and working condition. I also had to get counseling to assist me in sorting the negative barriers I associated with being a wife in the first place. With all of that in place, I now feel 100% more confident entering into a marriage as a wife.

If you are going to embark on this path of whole self-confidence and high esteem, you first need to have a sense of humor about your mistakes and be willing and open to real change. If you also own a business, or work, it is even more important to prioritize correctly.

Newsflash:

Husbands and wives are a priority (together) over jobs and kids (we will talk about that in my next book) (

Snapshot of a Confident Relationship:

1. A confident relationship allows each individual person to express him or herself freely. I remember my spiritual dad talking about acquiring the ability to love someone regardless of their performance. This message stuck with me throughout the course of my life because that is the exact opposite of what we do. We women are particularly good at finding fault in character and situation and it's not fair to the men in our lives. Nor is it fair in any of our other friendships, professional relationships, or otherwise. Learning to have a healthy high esteem as an individual takes care of this problem most of the time because as confident individuals we learn how to accept that everyone else is also a work in progress. Logically, we know that there are no perfect people. Realistically, we hold people to a standard and don't even realize it.

A confident relationship manages and deals with issues as they arise with immediate forgiveness for the other person and a mutual understanding that issues don't necessarily have to be resolved, just understood and maintained.

In order to possess the boldness and freedom that a confident relationship has to offer, we have to learn to let go of the previous relationships where they did not work and we failed. We must forgive ourselves, render anything worth rendering and move forward

Chapter Thirteen – Confidence is for Relationships

with confidence and a newfound respect for other people in the same way that we desire to be respected and understood. We need our actions to speak so loudly that no one can really hear what we say.

1. A confident relationship adds value to our lives. Unfortunately, we are not Jesus. Therefore, the accepting and embracing of all people no matter what takes on a different meaning for us. Our human structure is only designed to carry so much. When we push those limits we run the risk of faster wear and tear, and unnecessary damage.

While working in property management, it took me a long time to logically understand why six people couldn't fit into a large two bed-room unit. Because I am a creative, I could've artistically created enough living and sleeping space that would allow a large accommodation. What I learned is that a two bedroom apartment is built with materials, design, and foundational structure based on two bodies. Overstepping that limit would not only cause normal wear and tear to happen sooner, but the entire foundation could be shifted and therefore cause major destruction.

Our structure is no different. We do not have enough time in a day, week, month, or year to tend to the thousands of people that we will meet and actually like in our lifetime. This is why it is important to recognize why we may meet someone. Sometimes, it's just for a purpose or season and once the season is over or purpose complete we need to let go. We have a hard time with this because we see it more as rejection than filtering.

Just like the two-bedroom apartment, we are not built to hold onto too many people. We need to figure out who adds value that can be recycled over a long period of time. Once that value is enough we then put someone else in their place and allow them to add value to someone else. This is how we effectively manage relationships. Jesus started with many, ended up with twelve, and died with three.

The only exception to this rule and we are definitely at the very least designed to merge with at least one other for life.

Our spouse.

1. A confident relationship never uses children, money, or new relationship as a weapon. For us women this is probably the hardest hurdle to overcome. It was for me. It's not that we are bad people because of it. We have a multi-functional job when it comes to relationships, giving birth, protecting our children and ourselves all while battling previous experiences with brokenness and not fully healing from it, hormonal changes in the body before, during, and after pregnancy and a maternal instinct to protect what we create.

What we have to learn to do as women is to separate and sort feelings from circumstances. While this is definitely not an easy thing to master it is absolutely possible with the heart of a willing participant.

In these situations we need to learn to keep other people out of the equation. I love this quote by Joyce Meyer:

"Have no opinion where you have no responsibility"

I write this in my blogs and journals all the time as a reminder and teacher of how damaging unsolicited advice can be.

Chapter Thirteen – Confidence is for Relationships

Once we learn to keep others out of our business, we can allow ourselves to fully engage in an accept the situation for what it is, wrap our mind around what is truly best practice for everyone involved, and come up with a sensible peaceful solution. We were built for that. I did it, so I know that it is possible and if you allow me to, I will show you how.

At the end of the day a confident relationship offers peace and tranquility. Enough to restore the fire for tomorrow's battle. At the end of the day a confident relationship is a peaceful one.

Even if that means no relationship in this season of your life.

Healthy breaks are not only permitted, but encouraged.

Do you need to take one?

Chapter Fourteen – Confidence Eliminates Bullying

Bullying is not a new trend. It is an old and growing problem so severe that no one wants to face it; yet we want to protect ourselves and our kids from it by fighting it from a distance or fighting its sub-issue. The sub-issue of bullying is focusing solely on the person causing the harm while knowing the reality is that we will never be able to control someone else's behavior. It won't work. No matter how we expose a child, parent or employer to the behavior of hurting or harassing someone, their logic isn't going to scream "wow, your right I *am* being a bully, let me stop this unacceptable behavior".

As a community, we are confused as to why individuals and groups continue to bully as if they were not exposed to its danger in the first place. The child that harasses another child verbally or physically sits in the principal's office awaiting discipline. The executive that is under investigation for sexual harassment of his ex-girlfriend, who also happens to work with him, takes a paid leave of absence and spends a little time on the beach. The teenage boy that confides in another adult family member about the verbal and controlling behavior of his parent is told that it's normal during the teen years and to do whatever the parent says because it's for their best interest.

Let's change the angle so that your mind can begin to open itself up to different perceptions. A nine-year-old is continually causing a disruption in class. He is verbally harassing another student by name calling. He used to be friends with the other student but after an altercation in math, that friendship dissolved. The parents of the student being called names voice their anger and want something done immediately because they view it as bullying. It turns out that the father of the child causing the disruption is an alcoholic. When the child comes home from school he is beaten on most nights, screamed at for getting in trouble again, and then told to toughen up by his alcohol-driven father. His mother stands by and says or does nothing. Now he cannot return to that school due to expulsion. The child he harasses is a girl.

We blame the bully.

Let's put a suit on it so you can see the same problem in a different wardrobe. The executive that is under investigation for sexual harassment just got a promotion for his leadership and dedication. He assumed that he and his ex-girlfriend (now subordinate) were on good terms because she was nice to him. The executive began to date another woman. The romance took flight and he asked his new girlfriend to marry him. When his ex-girlfriend found out that he proposed to his new fiancé, she became jealous and wanted him back.

She'd always find a way to be alone in a room with him to make sexual gestures. He assertively declined. With his strong and direct communication skills he explains to the ex-girlfriend that he loves

Chapter Fourteen – Confidence Eliminates Bullying

his fiancé and that if they are to continue to have an employment relationship that her behavior has to stop immediately or he would have to report her. This makes the ex-girlfriend feel rejected so she files a sexual harassment claim and it gets leaked to the media. His fiancé finds out and leaves him.

We blamed the bully.

A teenage boy confides in a family member that his coach is calling him names. He repeatedly makes him stay after practice to put in extra work to "toughen him up" because coach found out he was gay. He isn't sure if he can trust a family member enough to talk to them about his new sexual orientation or coach without his mother finding out. He decides to confide in his cousin. His cousin breaches trust and tells his mother. She is disappointed in him and blames herself for her son's sexual orientation because his father was not around. His mother then forces him to continue to play on the basketball team and threatens him by withholding food and shelter if he doesn't comply. The situation with coach gets worse. After all of the other boys are gone from the locker room he performs oral sex on the boy and tells him that he won't be so hard on him as long as he doesn't tell a soul. Why would he? The boys in the locker room always talk derogatorily about faggots and gays. Eventually, the teenage boy commits suicide.

Who do we blame?

I call these surface issues because the layer that gets the most attention is the top one. As a culture we deal with action and reaction better than we do cause and effect. I declare a change in perception and behavior. I'm not a huge advocate of mediation or bringing together an agreement between perpetrator and victim. The platform is uneven, unfair, and the behavior still needs to be addressed.

However, if we began to train in the areas of self-worth and confidence this will give the bullies and manipulators a rough time. Confident people respect their self-worth. They grow from tribulation and they are excellent communicators.

Bullies can't bully self-confidence.

Bullying isn't this new idea that's causing problems all of a sudden. It is not restricted to the schoolyard and it is definitely not a youth only problem. The word "bullying" itself isn't even sufficient enough to describe its nature because it has such a wide range of definitions, elements, and layers that describing it in one word isn't profound enough to cause an impact on one's ears.

To try and define bullying would be limitless and subjective. Just in the way that a bully threatens and intimidates another child in a school setting, so does an authority figure or parent when creating a fearful, intimidating environment for their children where they cannot grow and flourish. Although those examples highlight two different environments, the bullying is still the same.

Its last name: Abuse.

Who Is Responsible

We are. Bullying doesn't just affect us as individuals; it influences the discernment in our many types of relationships. We sit passively and allow the controlling behavior of our companions dictate who we talk to and where go by always being available and responsive at the hip on our smartphones. This is an example of relationship bullying. Our management at work conducts meetings full of screaming, mandatory paid lunch training seminars, and threatens

CHAPTER FOURTEEN – CONFIDENCE ELIMINATES BULLYING

our jobs, citing lack of focus from the team. This is harassment alive and well in the workplace.

Now that our careers are on the line and our relationship demands more time than what it's worth we lose mental energy and can't focus on our children. Instead, we scream, instill fear, neglect our kids, and demand that they be perfect hoping that they don't turn out like we did. In return, they don't thrive and grow. They walk on eggshells until they are of age and we never hear from them again. This is parental bullying.

Our priorities are out of whack because the cycle of silence and passivity has always transcended. Our communities are confused. According to Dan Olweus from the National School Safety Centers, American schools harbor approximately 2.1 million bullies and 2.7 million of their victims. They are shocked to learn that bullying statistics say *revenge* is the strongest motivation for school shootings and an astounding 87% of shootings are motivated by a desire to "get back at those who have hurt them." After the confusion and shock comes the anger and rage in a community when there is an "incident" that affects the masses. Harassment and bullying have been linked to 75% of school-shooting incidents.

We are initiating a war with the wrong weapons and we are trying to win by finger pointing and blaming instead of taking personal responsibility for our individual development, confidence building, and passing that along to our children for their reference and identity. If our schedules don't permit time to prepare a home cooked meal for our children and we chose a business meeting over school recital, we are sending our children onto the battlefield fatigued and wearing ballet slippers. If our goals are wealth and success rather than time and love, then we harbor the largest, most expensive, weapon of mass destruction and leave the red button with no instruction manual to a rich generation with no character.

Individuals who commit disturbing crimes were once victims themselves. Our emotional programming resorts to sympathy before empathy because we are designed to care for and serve others. When havoc occurs, it shakes and shocks us. We become permanent screen fixtures because destruction has interrupted our idea and plan for life, forcing us to accept that our fate is not in our control. Our question then becomes "who has control of our life then?" Our second question is contrary to the first because we ask, "How can one human have a right to another's fate?"

Murder causes an impact. Rape causes an impact. Racial discrimination, terrorism, suicide, parricide and child abuse are all words that cause impact. What I will step forward and boldly declare is that aside from murder– only because of its permanence– all of those other words fall under "bullying."

Advocacy

Bullying and abuse have long term affects. The younger it begins the most impact it will have. It is said and proven that victims of bullying later create victims. According to bullying statistics 2010, there are about 2.7 million students being bullied each year by about 2.1 students taking on the role of the bully. It's possible that your child is likely to one or the other.

It is hard to think that your child is responsible for bullying someone or could be a victim. People would rather watch reality television, than to hear about a sexual predator in the neighborhood, an alcoholic father, or molester in the family. It makes us uncomfortable knowing something so horrid can also be very close to home.

Chapter Fourteen – Confidence Eliminates Bullying

We place "those types of people" in their own compartment in our minds. We feel like we can't relate to those types of situations yet those situations are actually happening at our family reunions and in the basement of our houses. The sexual predator didn't just branch out into the streets and decide to look for new victims; he probably started out as the alcoholic father and family molester. But because we didn't put him away, his territory spread. Now he is responsible for multiple rapes in various cities and hard to locate and capture.

You and I share a mutual connection. We harbor secrets so deep that we stop believing in the truth of its existence. We have pushed these secrets so far into the core of our lives that even when there is a possibility of it surfacing we can effectively, thoroughly, and subconsciously avoid the triggers.

I was fortunate. I made it to the other side of the fence. A lot of you who were once or are currently victims of bullying and abuse don't make it through to this side of the fence, where you can accept that you are not at fault. Some of you want the permission to heal, forgive, and restore the foundation of your internal worthiness but you don't allow time for process. Instead to add layers of extra non-important junk on the surface of your true calling because of fear or you run. You run as far and fast as possible because crossing that fence means that other people will have an opportunity to judge you. You care too much what other people might say not realizing that it is only on the other side of that fence that you will ever truly be your most authentic you.

On this side of the fence your senses are heightened. You will become more in tuned to how you think, feel and behave. Your hearts will grow stronger and wisdom will penetrate deeper than the root of a grey hair strand. This self-refined philosophy molds you to be better parents, leaders and individuals. This side of the fence is where you will find true peace. True peace is life altering.

If you chose to stay submersed in victim disposition you will become permanently screwed up and no one ever really gets to hear or be inspired by your story. You will remain afraid, timid, and manipulated into believing that keeping those secrets inside of you will protect you like it always has. Because of that fear, the people who struggle after you will never get the blueprint of how to overcome. Those victims will never receive the memo that there is a way out, which they can fight to gain back.

It's hard to admit to the long term or life altering effects of our past issues. I get that our actions have consequences that affect our current situation. We become silent because of the fear of losing our jobs, shaking the status quo in our families, and suffering from old wounds. I get it.

We'd rather go through life fast and easy just to get through it, while taking blows and submitting to its mundane functions. We take jobs that don't speak to our purpose but put money in our pockets and food on our tables, believing that that's how life is supposed to be.

But it's not.

We watch the news about another child committing suicide over a social media post and shake our heads quietly hoping and praying that it doesn't happen to our children. How cowardly have we become to point the finger at the child who bullies mocks and pokes fun at the child who appears to be weaker? Have we forgotten that the bully himself is a child who is practicing learned behavior and is in need of guidance and support?

Chapter Fourteen – Confidence Eliminates Bullying

Life can be simple, but its lessons are not. We cannot continue to just stand by and watch the epidemic of bullying continue to take over.

We are born.

We learn.

We grow.

We work.

We give birth.

We die.

Yet there is always something on the inside of us that yearns to reach out for more. The question haunts us every time a shift is made in our lives-"is this what I'm made for?" By the time we ponder the question long enough to think about making a change, we get sucked back in to the habit of life and all of its stress and worry. That question remains in our secret place only to reveal itself when there is a tragedy in our lives or quiet time beyond our control. Most of the time, it's too late. We have already been sucked dry, angered out, diagnosed or fed up.

I am here to pull that question out of the shadows and into the light as frequent and necessary as you need for implementation. It's time for you to hop back on the boat of your mind and remember your stories, struggles, traumas and issues of life. Once you gather them, you then bring them back to shore, sort them and figure out how you can help someone else.

Do you think it is easy for me to share with the world that I took my own mother's life? Do you think that it was easy for me to dig, research, and make peace with her life ending the way it did? I am here to tell you that it was far from easy. I had to go through the process of mourning her loss as a child while facing the punishment for her death.

I went back to drag the skeletons out of my closet to show yours up. To let you know that there is nothing too great or too horrid that you can't overcome. I went back to the reality of my past, alone and afraid. I dug through the dirt, endured the painful memories, journaled, talked with multiple professionals, and prayed.

I regained my confidence as a woman by first accepting that I would never be a perfect one. I finally have the courage and nerve to step out and tell my side of the story! With certainty and boldness, I can say that what I have endured and what I have done will never define who I am. When examining my skeletons, if you see one that kind of looks like one of yours, you are more than welcome to borrow its marrow, the lessons that can be learned from it, so that you too can finally be who you were meant to be.

As I mentioned earlier, there are about 2.7 million students being bullied each year by about 2.1 students taking on the role of the bully. Have you ever been abused or bullied? Do you know someone who is or was?

Raw experience is the mother of all teachers. There is a form of validation that lives inside of you after going through wilderness. You were not sure if you would make it out alive and undamaged but when you did, the sense of humility and relief is overwhelming. What you have conquered pleads with you to reach out and share the strategy with other people who are now on the battlefield. It is selfish and unfair not to. Trying to void that wilderness experience

Chapter Fourteen – Confidence Eliminates Bullying

will cause a life of low self-worth and instability. The consequences are fatal for those who await your help and unnecessary hardship for yourself because you are walking outside of your purpose.

Chapter Fifteen – Confidence in Fear

As a previous flight attendant it was imperative to project confidence in these three scenarios in the event of a disaster.

1. The captain calls the cabin while in flight and informs the flight attendant that an engine is damaged and to prepare for an emergency landing. As a flight attendant, we take in the information with confidence showing no signs of panic. We hang up the phone, brief the other flight attendants, and prepare the cabin for the emergency landing.

2. We explain to the passengers that we are going to have an emergency landing and assist them with the oxygen mask as they deploy assisting those who are panicking.

3. After we have done step 1 and 2, while the plane is going down, we have to appear confident and comforting, while making sure that everyone is strapped in with their oxygen mask on. Then we take our jump seat, strapping ourselves in last while we wait what may be the end of our lives.

Our fear and confidence building process began while we were still toddlers. We watched our parents, mimicked them, and then sought approval for our efforts. When parents give that approval or praise regardless of its successfulness, it plants a seed of confidence. That is called concentrated confidence not watered down drips of affirmation.

How many times have you witnessed or even said to your child, "I just don't want you to end up like me" or, "I want you to be a better adult that I am". This is possibly the worst thing we can say as parents. I was guilty of it myself until I realized that that's the point. The mimicking toddler, the girl who watches mom put on make-up and heels, the boy who watches dad mow the lawn and go to work. Our children are supposed to be a replica of who we are, how we function, and what we do. It is in us that they find their values and worth and learn what they believe. It is now appropriate and crucial that we change our statements to our young boys and girls. We need to say to them, "Watch me, so that you can learn". If we do not begin this affirmation, our children will never understand who they are and will always turn to Google for the answer. When we teach values and boundaries and demonstrate confidence to our kids we become the filter for let's say–Google

It's never too late. Before we can begin to shape our leaders of tomorrow, we have to first instill that confidence in ourselves. Maybe our parents didn't do a good job of that for us. Maybe we have been abused and it destroyed the confidence that should've been growing strong on the inside of us all along. Chances are we thought we could put on the suit of confidence so that we could get by. We wear it when necessary and take it off when we are alone and behind closed doors because it is only an add-on and doesn't really exist on the inside of us. However, when we are caught off guard by a trigger involving self-confidence, it shows. Once it shows, we

Chapter Fifteen – Confidence in Fear

feel inadequate and un-worthy. The problem is that we never do anything about it. Today, that will no longer be the case. Our childhood may not have been the best. We may have gone through some things that rocked our existence, but we are here.

Somehow, some way, we made it here to this point and we look back and say "wow, not so bad for what I've been through". Our degrees, our children, our careers and our accomplishments somehow compensate for the inner confidence that we lack. Whatever it took to get us to this point is well appreciated because we know that it could've been worse and just like sever turbulence on an aircraft, we may understand what's happening at the time, but we also have in the back of our minds the thankfulness that the worse didn't happen.

Conclusion of Part Two

The simple things in life grab my attention the most. This entire process of designing this training to writing a book about it is summed up in a neat little package. What you don't realize is the amount to stress over-nighters and diaper change interruptions it took to get through it. I mean, even my smartphone was in danger of being thrown out of the window.

The key word here though is "process". Everything worth having or doing has one. My hope for you is that you embrace yours.

Part Three – The "Grounded in Confidence" Platform

Chapter Sixteen – Tools for Rebuilding Confidence

The reason I chose tools as a relationship to building self-confidence is because I wanted to make it simple and very easy to relate to. I wanted to create a visual, tangible action in comparison to a changed mindset or habit. There had to be dramatics because that's how most of us women are.

When I speak, or do a seminar on the tools, I have props that shock and startle my audience because I feel like if they remember the tool, they will also get the tools subliminal message. The rebuilding tools are an easy, thought-provoking idea. The real change though, is seen in the implementation of their purpose.

The platform of this training is simple; you get what you put in. I say, go hard. What else are you doing? Playing around on You Tube? What about that business? What about that career and family? Let's start on our journey of rebuilding the self-confidence we truly desire.

Tool Summary

The very first tool that I mastered and that I will teach you is represented by the saw. This tool aids in the process of destroying the box. Yep. The one everyone keeps trying to get you to think outside of. Its destruction is necessary because even a metaphorical box has sides which mean you have to be in one in order to look or think outside of it. My philosophy is to rid the box altogether. I am not advocating the absence of boundaries—in fact, I will teach you how to effectively create those too. What I need from you as a man or woman is open mindedness to a new idea. At one point no one could fathom being able to watch video on their cellular phone until one person did, and made it happen. This is the shift I am headed towards.

The second tool is represented by the shovel. This aids in the process of digging deep in the past where the ground is moist and bringing some of that soil to the present to mix with the dry soil so the dry soil can remember what it's supposed to feel like. This process is the most uncomfortable because you are opening old wounds. But I believe in you. Old wounds that are opened and cleansed usually heal with less complication and no visual scar. For me, this process required a team of people that I could go to when things got bad. I had a therapist, a minister in my church, and my best friend on speed dial, and, of course, a box of tissues. We will talk about how this process is crucial to the last three.

The third tool is identified by the magnifying glass. This aids in the process of evaluation of self. Knowing who we really are is the only way to make the desired revisions to become who we were meant to be. Our life's purpose isn't assigned to us. We don't just wake up one day and answer the door to purpose. We decide, design and mold what we are to become, but we first have to know what we are working with.

The fourth tool is the blank canvas. This represents a full spectrum

Chapter Sixteen – Tools for Rebuilding Confidence

of white space that gives you permission to design your new, revised self. This tool is exciting because it's all up to you. The redesign of you can be as extreme or modest as you want and guess what? There are no limits. You can change your physical self, your image, and you can understand and enhance your personality. I had a little help with this tool too because after leaving the institution, I had no real identity or idea who I was. Inside of the walls of the facility, I had a number, was identified by a crime and a place where others like me were housed. When I turned twenty-one all of those identifiers was taken away. This step is the core of your confidence training.

The last tool is a cloak. This tool represents a sealant. The cloak isn't a protector for the outside; it is designed as a reminder to protect the results of the other tools that you customized for your life. This is the tool you picture when you face adversity and self-doubt creeps in. This is a covering for your individuality and should not be taken lightly.

I designed these tools as a representation of a system that took me years to master. Aside from being stuck with the shovel for what seemed like forever, I had a really hard time re-creating myself with the graphite pencil. I'd press too hard—it would break, when it broke—it smeared and when it smeared it messed up the canvas I was trying to create. This resulted in dead-end relationships, unplanned pregnancies, and a variety of unrelated jobs to satisfy the short term need of an identity.

Are You Still Here?

If you are still with me on this journey, I commend you and have overwhelming respect for you. Not everyone has the heart to change because change is not easy. As a world overflowing with new ideas and evolving technology, we have figured out short cuts to everything and have taken it to extreme measures.

"Easy" is killing our health, children, and purpose. How many times do we need to go through a drive through to feed our kids before we realize that is exactly what is killing them? How miserable and depressed do we have to be before we chose a job or start a business that will cause us to love our work while living comfortably in our means? How many suicides are we going to see in our lifetime before switching on the gift on the inside of us that can reach out to those who cannot see the light at the end of the tunnel?

The final section of this book is going to offer you very tangible and workable "first steps" that will put you on the path to evaluating who you really are and what you really have to offer that you have buried so deep inside of your being that sometimes you can't even recognize whether or not it exists. You will be amazed at the level of understanding and wisdom you will embrace during this season of your journey. It will shock, scare, and even amaze you.

I have lived and worked in the structure of these tools for over fifteen years. I didn't realize they were an aid to my growth and learning until I started to get results. Those results were extraordinary and I felt honored to piece things together the way that I did to get the desired results I needed. When my peers began to ask me for advice, I had some to give. When they too started getting their desired results, I felt proud and the desire to teach others grew more. It's not that I am smarter, or better that anyone else. I have had the opportunity to go through a period of uninterrupted learning that no one else would have been able to without extenuating circumstances. These processes based on that learning have been developed

Chapter Sixteen – Tools for Rebuilding Confidence

and tested over time. My desire was to make them relevant, interesting, and easy to apply. The actual tools have been on Earth forever. They have real purpose and are designed to complete a task. Therefore, when you are applying their metaphorical use to your training, you will have an actual tool that represents the symbolic reference.

This new systematic way of developing a strong sense of self, high confidence, and esteem will give you relief. Re-building your self-confidence doesn't have to be a long, difficult process. The results will stem from the amount of heart you put into it. The good news is that no matter the amount you put in, there will be real and visible change because I am going to show you how to build from the foundation of who you already are to get to what you want to be. This is your upgrade, your new and improved software that will allow you to move through life seamlessly and in purpose.

As children, we didn't have a choice; we had to trust those who were placed in authority over us. Whether it was a system, blood, or a Good Samaritan we had to accept what they told us about ourselves and the world around us. We had no choice but to love the people they loved and dislike those whom they disliked.

The biggest and most important part of this re-building process now is that we have a choice and a say in what is in our foundation and from that, we will grow new roots and those new roots become our new tree of life.

So, I'm ready, if you are.

When people ask me how I became so confident after what appears like an impossible life, I can give true and accurate information by introducing this method, be extremely accurate when doing so, and teach you so that you can immediately reap the benefits of being a confident individual and not have to enroll and study inside the school of hard-knocks like I did.

As any other expert in the personal development arena, I want to make very clear that this method, or any for that matter, is not a guarantee. I simply cannot guarantee happiness, contentment, riches, or even confidence. Not only would it go completely against best practices, but I know better than anyone that everything you learn will only have the effect on you that you permit. Everyone has a different learning style, personality, determination, and life experience, so the application of a training system will have different results for everyone.

What will set you apart is your heart. Are you willing to risk familiar for new and improved? Are you willing to step out of your comfort zone and consider a new view? Are you really ready for a change that goes beyond your surface need into the infrastructure of your heart?

If you answered "yes" to those questions, then you are the boldest and most driven person in the world right now.

Oprah ain't got nothing on you.

The tools offered in this book are a compacted version of the lessons I have learned from experience, counseling, other individuals, and trial and error. My stories seem so far out and unreal that I look back myself and wonder, how did I survive that? I lived out of my car in California as a flight attendant when I wasn't on the jet, I was lost on the streets of New York, lived in a homeless shelter in downtown Cleveland, Ohio and here I am now. My kids and I are ok, with no blemishes or wounds.

Chapter Sixteen – Tools for Rebuilding Confidence

Right now, some of you may be on the brink of greatness and all you need is a push. You will read and study the tools here and take off into a whole new you and completely change your future. Others may require a little more understanding of the process and deeper internal practice. For you, my book Grounded in Confidence and the workbook along with it will seamlessly compliment *From the Ground Up*. This digs deeper into the confidence training and tools to allow for more focused perception and more practice with application. There is no risk to try because I personally believe that if you embrace these processes, they will change your life.

They did mine.

Chapter Seventeen – Roadblocks Ahead

As your narrating coach and trainer on this epic journey I promise you that you will hit major roadblocks during this process. In fact, there are three that I know you will encounter for sure and I want to offer some encouragement and tactics to help you tear down these walls that are purposely designed to stop your growth and cause you misery for as long as you live.

"A roadblock is only a temporary barrier -a checkpoint designed to measure your agility to ensure you are truly ready to cross over to the next level"

Roadblock One: The monster at the end of this book.

I realize that I am definitely giving away my age when I say this. When I was little there was a book that I always read. It was a part of the Little Golden Book Collection® that featured the puppets of Sesame Street. The title of it is *The Monster at the End of this Book*. Now, stay with me because this is important. I would even dare to request that if you have not read this childhood favorite or you're young enough to make fun of those of us who have—purchase it. The book was funny, colorful and easy to read as a child, but the revelation you can receive from it as an adult is priceless.

Grover, the blue guy on the front of the book greets the reader with excitement and anticipation. As if he jumped the gun and didn't realize it, he gets to the next page and realizes what the name of the book was. He spends each page begging a pleading for readers not to turn to the next page because of the fact that there is a monster at the end. Grover is very dramatic in trying to convince the readers not to keep turning the page. He uses tactics and materials like ropes and nails that will seemingly stop readers from turning the page.

When readers turn the page it's as if they destroy the set up that Grover worked so hard to create. The final tactic that Grover uses is a brick wall and he is convinced that the reader will be unable to turn the page. Once the page is turned and bricks are destroyed Grover realizes that no matter what the reader is going to reveal the monster at the end. At this point, all Grover can do is beg and plead his case. He talks about how afraid he is and all the danger that lies ahead because of our turning of the pages. Grover knew the end of the book was going to eventually come. He knew the entire time that there was a monster at the end. When he realized that he was the monster, I'm sure that's not why he was disappointed. I believe that he was disappointed that he spent all that time fighting against it, being afraid of it, and coming to the conclusion that it was him all along.

We are no different than Grover as we begin this journey of re-inventing and re-establishing the very heart of what the rest of our life can be like. Just like Grover, we jump head first and take risks on journeys that tugged at our heart or reached us emotionally, while not fully focusing on the level of difficulty it can bring. But then it's too late! We have already purchased the program, signed up for the

Chapter Seventeen – Roadblocks Ahead

training, entered the relationship or committed to the event. At this point we have two options. We can immediately turn around and go back, get a refund, or break a heart. Or, we can go forward— afraid as hell but moving, believing in the gut feeling that brought us to this place.

What I noticed about Grover is that even though he was afraid, he went on with the journey kicking, screaming and pleading along the way. The thing is, he probably endured more injury and suffering during the process because of the fear.

Like Grover, we are taking a risk with this new journey. This risk will involve very deep personal feelings and belief examinations that scare us so much that we may not want to turn to the next page or move on to the next step. In fact, we may get held back at times or may not progress as fast as we would like to because of this particular roadblock.

There is good news and bad news when it comes to the monster at the end of this book. The bad news is the fear of unknown is one of the greatest fears that can disrupt any process. This is why people give up before they even began. But this is not going to be true for you because you now have an advantage against the fear.

Awareness.

One benefit of beginning any personal development or improvement journey is the fact that we are doing something. To just think about change or even want it bad enough is not forward movement and if it were easy, everyone would do it. If we keep pushing through we may find that sometimes, we get overly anxious about nothing and like Grover, the monster at the end of the book is you. So how do we get through roadblock one?

Don't allow "you" to get in the way of your journey.

Roadblock Two: Smooth Criminals

Have you ever met anyone who can talk their way out of anything? The problem with this roadblock is those people can also talk you out of your own growth and development. These will be close relatives and friends that are seemingly offering their good advice or the "cares so much about you that they don't want to see you disappointed" conversation. While the people in your life mean well and are not purposely trying to ruin your life, they are.

I label them as smooth criminals because they don't realize how much damage they are causing you by offering their two cents. In both the close knit community of our most intimate relationships to the outbursts of friends in our social networking we subconsciously seek the approval of others. Long gone are the days of facial expression warnings and head-shaking disapprovals. The dependency has become so obvious that we have been reduced to looking forward to thumbs up but never get the thumbs down option.

Getting through this roadblock is the easiest and hardest first step on your journey to confidence. It's easy because your venture is custom made to fit you which means you will understand and process in your own unique way. It will be difficult because as with any new and improved thing, we want it to shine. We want to show the world that we are worthy of "new and improved".

The first thing we tend to do is announce our intention. We talk about it all the time and to anyone who will listen. The issue with that is that "Smooth Criminals" are family, friends and coworkers, who may not be able to understand why you need this training in

Chapter Seventeen – Roadblocks Ahead

the first place and may say something out of his or her emotional bank and cause you to think twice about cashing your check.

Think of this roadblock as a diamond in the making. At this current level, you are only pure carbon matter and really no different than anyone else. You still have to be burnt, shaped and cut and that process may not be pretty at all. Whether your process includes completing a journey, starting a business, or improving a skill, you want to shout it out to the world that your finished product will shine with brilliance.

Yet you secretly wonder, will it?

The announcement you make to others isn't about making everyone else aware of the journey ahead and inviting them to celebrate your upcoming victory. It's because, subconsciously, we want their approval.

We don't need it.

As hard as it will be to not hang the *work in progress* sign on the door on the way out, it will be well worth the restraint when someone says to you "There's something different about you, what is it?"— that will be your green light and confirmation that something is happening.

Roadblock Three: Ready? Get Set. Stop.

You're strolling with your customized latte in one hand and electronic device in the other and it catches your attention as if it stepped right out in front of you; the "How to" guide for getting the love of your life back. It's like fate because you had been thinking about them a lot more than usual within the past few days. You then decide that there is no better time than now to get them back. By the time you measure their worth and relationship with you against your wallet you have not only bought the guide, but the t-shirt and calendar as well because at that very moment you realize the most important concept there is to realize about relationships-they are priceless

You think about them the entire drive home because where you felt there was no hope is now an entire training manual to aid you in your endeavor. You are in love with the idea of the end result before even getting started in the process.

Until you arrive home.

You clear the table, grab your notebook and with butterflies fluttering on the inside of you, you are pumped and ready for whatever step one is because you really want to get back what you lost. You began reading the very first step in getting back the love you lost. Step one:

Apologize.

As you read this very first, and obviously crucial, step you find your energy level going from highly caffeinated to extremely low. Although you may love them and really miss that relationship, trying to get them back seems as if it's going to take a whole lot of work. Right off, the very first step is something you don't feel like you should have to do.

Wow, you think to yourself. *I didn't think it would be this hard. Maybe I should wait until I'm in a better place in my life. Maybe I won't have time. Maybe—*

Chapter Seventeen – Roadblocks Ahead

Your mind drifts off into this never ending sea of possible roadblocks before you even started and before you know it, your caffeine high has been reduced to sandman dust, you yawn and give yourself permission to give up. All within a short period of time you have talked yourself out of something that at one point meant everything to you. Although that is just an example, it's pretty much how we deal with things.

Emotionally and irresponsibly.

Thing is, we don't realize it, until it's too late.

Emotional drain will destroy desire quicker than a burning flame.

Personal development or confidence re-building is not a new "thing". But how many times have you started a program and not finished? How many things have you not seen through to the end because something happened to change your focus or because it was emotionally draining from the start?

I have. Numerous times.

Some of those things I went back to, some I did not. But the key is pushing past the point of discouragement, through the physical drain of emotional control and onto the victory that you so deserve.

This is the only roadblock that is seemingly contradicting because it was the "ready" that prompted you and got you pumped up for the end result before you even got started. "Set" was just waiting for a shot and was cheering you on because the middle man "set" has nothing to lose. All "set" does is wait for the signal to take off. This area is where we overthink and under-consider what it is that we need. We will make so many excuses in this part of our roadblock because there is stalling. But the problem with most of us is that "go" never comes. We never grant ourselves full permission to take care of ourselves the way we take care of other people. The concept is foreign and the risk is great because taking care of ourselves means giving into an idea that will cause change in our lives. As old and true as it is, this saying kills dreams and weakens talent every single day:

"If it were easy, everybody would do it."

So here is my solution to you for this roadblock. Recognize it and accept it for the distraction that it is. Be prepared for it and sit and wait for it as if you are geared up for the biggest race in your life. This race plays such a vital part in how you will move on to the next phase of your life that the preparation is built to weed out the weak.

But not you.

You have come too far and worked too hard to get this far. Here you sit at the starting line. Yes, you could back out now, yes, you could change your mind and go back to life as you know it. But there is something about your expectation. There is something about the possibility of the end turning out just as or better than you expected. This is your moment.

You have helped other people reach their moment. You have come early, stayed late and taken plenty for the team. You have been walked on, used, taken advantage of and overlooked and now here you stand at your breakthrough.

How do you overcome this road block?

Get Ready.

Chapter Seventeen – Roadblocks Ahead

You accept that it won't be easy. Expect distractions, orange cones, and the chastisement of other people. Accept the disclaimers and warning labels for what they are. Information.

Get Set.

Prepare. Shift and move things around so that your journey fits you comfortably. Gather what you think you may need but don't be surprised if other needs arise. Get weird. Talk to yourself, write on your mirrors, make encouraging post-it notes, and shake it off. Place your ear buds in your ear, hit play and

Go.

Once you are here, turning back won't be an option. No one will have to tell you that.

Epilogue

What's crazy is that there used to be a whole other section to this book. I actually went into the details of the training, tools and assignments. The feedback I received was, in summary, "Whoa Tammy Jo, overload. Just write two books." When I went back through my manuscript, I had to agree. There was so much information that I wanted to get to you, that I just over did it. So "Grounded in Confidence" is the spinoff. The actual confidence training.

On another note, I am honored that people are in awe of me. I am honored to be such an inspiration. I believe that there is no other reason why I came through what I did.

Standing here is a miracle that could only have God as the founder. I have dedicated my entire life to being a true example of how God feels about those He loves and what He can do if we just allow Him in. I'm not talking about dead, fake, confused infested, customized religion.

I'm talking about God exchanging my human flaws, allowing my catastrophes to illuminate His presence while loving His beautiful, good, sinless, crown of the earth (me) enough to give His only begotten Son, so that I would not perish, but have eternal life.

I'd say it's a win-win.

If you want to experience that kind of love by Him, all you have to do is pray this prayer out loud in the presence of God.

God, I am a mess in my own eyes.

I know that you created me and I am therefore a beautiful mess in your eyes. I am a sinner and very rarely do I get things right. I lie, cheat, and do things that you don't like. For those things, I am sorry.

Because you sent your Son, Jesus to die for all the wrong anyone could every do, it means that not only do I have a chance to live with you eternally, but that I am good.

Your Word says that if I confess my sins, you are faithful and just to forgive me *of my* sins, and will cleanse me from all unrighteousness.

I know that you also said in your Word that if I say that I have no sin, I am deceiving myself and the truth is not in me.

So here I am Lord, I am a sinner. I repent for anything I have done to offend you or anyone else. I confess that Jesus is Lord and that you raised Him from the dead for this purpose:

To have a shot at eternal life—with you.

Epilogue

I want that shot. I want you to come into my life and completely revamp me soul so that I can become more like you. I know I won't be perfect, but I will be good, and that's good enough. I may disappoint you sometime, I may mess up often, but I will always remember that I am now Yours and I want to be cleansed and used just like Tammy Jo. If you did it for her, I know you will for me.

Thank you for salvation, thank you for my new life.

In Jesus' name—Amen.

Now if you prayed that out loud, congratulations! As you begin on your journey with God know that you cannot change anything on your own accord. No one is really going to care about your new life more than you and others who understand what that means because they too have a relationship with God.

All you have to do is what anyone would do in a new relationship…build.

Remember, what you have done in your past doesn't matter to Him. Or you could even think of it like, you haven't done anything as seemingly worse than me and I'm forgiven.

My daughter put on her white dressing that covered her body, face mask, and cloth shower cap. She didn't say much but I knew she was excited. I figured with everything we had been through the months before, it would be a comfort to have her by my side. I could tell she was excited and anxious at the same time.

I on the other hand was a nervous wreck. I kept thinking to myself, *"Who does this all over again after nine years, and why am I".*

I kept thinking back to what other people were telling me I should do. They were giving me their opinion based on their own belief and life experiences. Abortion, adoption, and struggle were words that rand clear. If I would have listened to them, I would probably be depressed or guilt ridden. I'm really glad that I have the confidence to make decisions on my own and can pray and talk to God about any area or any situation that I may be in or facing.

She helped me to put on my gear that was identical to hers and we were taken to a very cold room. She sat beside me and I remember having this conversation with myself in my head:

You have to be strong for her. Show her that you can do this and that you can do it without fear. She is watching your every move.

I felt the first layer open. The second followed. There was tugging and pulling that I could not describe in words. I wasn't in pain. I was in amazement that my body was able to sustain and develop in this way.

Tears ran down the side of my eye and I couldn't contain myself. My daughter wiped my face and said, "Its ok mom, he is almost here".

Within moments, I heard a loud, wail coming from the bottom of the table. The doctor held up my son, clipped his umbilical cord, wrapped him in a blanket and handed him to my daughter. He quieted down and my daughter looked him in the face and smiled. That was the moment that I realized

I do have purpose.

Epilogue

And even though I may have changed things in my past and made better decisions, I was glad that I was given the opportunity to be a mother all over again. My mom did an awesome job in the values she instilled in me. Those values are what make up who I am as a person. What I did will never define who I am. I am a child of God and no one can ever take that away from me.

Not even me.

I was molested as a child, bullied in school and suffered from those things silently. At twelve years old in an attempt to take my own life, I shot and killed my mom instead. She wasn't supposed to die, I was. By sixteen, I cut on my arm, practiced satanic worship and decided that I no longer cared about life. By thirty-six, I had my third unplanned pregnancy, got married—then divorced, experienced homelessness in both Los Angeles and Cleveland but lived through it to talk about it. I've caused hurt and been heartbroken, frustrated and caused frustration, sick and sometimes mean. Once I made the decision to take control of my esteem and my life, I became healthy, confident and unstoppable.

My past will never define who I am.

Only I can do that.

The same goes for you.

What are you waiting for?

www.ingramcontent.com/pod-product-compliance
Lightning Source LLC
Chambersburg PA
CBHW031640040426
42453CB00006B/161